Earl and Nancy...
memories of our great
friend and past chair
of IHA Foundation
Tom Haggai
2008

John Montgomery Belk
1920–2007

THE WIT & WISDOM OF
JOHN MONTGOMERY BELK

Edited by Dr. Tony Zeiss

Central Piedmont Community College Press

Copyright ©2008 by Tony Zeiss

Commissioned by the Central Piedmont Community College Foundation
Charlotte, North Carolina
www.cpcc.edu/foundation

All rights reserved, no portion of this book may be reproduced or transmitted in any form or by any means except for brief quotations in reviews or articles without prior written permission of the publisher. Requests to the publisher for permission should be directed to Dr. Kevin McCarthy, CPCC Foundation, P. O. Box 35009, Charlotte, North Carolina, 28235-5009.

All net proceeds from the sale of this book will support the John and Claudia Belk Scholarship Fund at Central Piedmont Community College.

Published by the Central Piedmont Community College Press
Printed by Jostens
Charlotte, North Carolina

Library of Congress Cataloging-in-Publication Data
Zeiss, Paul Anthony, 1946-
The Wit and Wisdom of John Montgomery Belk/Tony Zeiss – 1st edition

FIRST EDITION
ISBN 978-1-59494-032-3

Reorder information:
CPCC Press
call 704-330-6789 or email cpccpress@cpcc.edu
www.cpcc.edu [Keyword: Press]

$20.00

ISBN 978-1-59494-032-3

❧ Contents ❧

Foreword   9

Introduction   11
    by Darrell E. Williams

Chapter One   17
    Memories from Family and Friends

Chapter Two   85
    John Belk's Wit

Chapter Three   97
    John Belk's Wisdom

Chapter Four   113
    Quoting John Montgomery Belk

Chapter Five   119
    Parting Thoughts

Appendix I   129

Appendix II   133

Appendix III   136

Appendix IV   139

Index   141

⇒ Foreword ⇐

Like thousands of other people, I loved John Belk. He had a rare blend of wit, wisdom, confidence, and humility which made him an exceptional leader and friend.

I knew he was a very special person from the time my wife, Beth, and I first met him in January of 1993. From that moment on, I kept all of his notes and cards, jotted down his anecdotes and jokes, and recorded his stories as he told them. It is an honor to be able to compile this tribute to John that represents a sampling of the fond memories held by his family and some of his closest friends. I thank Tommy Norman and Ralph Pitts for encouraging me to publish these memories.

Although John only stood five feet six inches tall and weighed 110 pounds as a sophomore at Charlotte Central High School, he grew to an imposing six feet four inches and 210 pounds by the time he entered Davidson College. He wasn't particularly articulate, but he found a way to communicate with impact, although it sometimes took days for that impact to dawn on the listener. John used to say that his friends told him he "couldn't lead a silent prayer." His humor was infectious and his wisdom was revered.

Alex Coffin, author of *Brookshire and Belk, Businessmen in City Hall,* gives this account of why John was so admired by the people of Charlotte:

"As he stepped down (from four terms as mayor), Belk received accolade after accolade and it was said in the newspaper editorials that he sought office 'out of a sense of duty, not ambition' and that he almost always showed 'good will, affection and good humor' while serving. Newspapers across the South took note not only of the end of the Belk administration, but also of the end of the businessman-as-mayor era. As he left office, he credited his father with being the greatest influence in his life . . ."

It was obvious to everyone that John Belk loved Charlotte and remained a grateful and humble man all of his life.

This book could not exist without the contributions of over seventy people who agreed to share some remembrance of their friend. Except for family members and John's administrative assistants, the position and sequence of the stories are randomly placed.

Scores of contributors told me they considered John Belk their best friend. And, from what I knew and have since learned about John, the feeling was reciprocal. John truly loved people, especially his family and those with whom he worked and socialized. It is a characteristic of extraordinary people to be thought of as the *best friend* of so many.

Several people told me their version of the same incident. John talked to so many people and his interactions were almost without number. Redundancy would not work well, so I elected to print the story that most closely fit with my own or Claudia's recollection. It is my hope that the contributors to this work will understand.

Every known means was taken to verify John's stories, incidents, and quotes and yet there is always the possibility for inaccuracy due to faulty memories and embellishments. In the event that such an error was made in these pages, it is hoped that forgiveness is granted. In the end, if this small book contributes to the lasting memory of John Montgomery Belk and if it helps a grieving family and community to be comforted in only a small way, its purpose will have been achieved.

A great debt of thanks is owed to Claudia Belk and Mary Claudia Pinon; each of the contributors of stories, anecdotes, and quotes; to Susan Oleson, Patricia McCaskill, Doug Cobb and Richard Griffin for their production expertise; to Darrell Williams for writing the Introduction; to the CPCC Press; and to the CPCC Foundation for funding this worthy project.

∼ INTRODUCTION ∽
by Darrell E. Williams
Belk, Inc. manager, executive communications

It was good fortune or perhaps Presbyterian predestination that brought me to Belk in June 1979, when I joined the company's communications department and first met John Belk. I had been working as editor of the Tarboro, North Carolina, *Daily Southerner* newspaper for several years when my wife Elizabeth, eager to return home to Charlotte, clipped a want ad from *The Charlotte Observer* advertising an opening at Belk under Ray Killian, the company's long-time head of human resources and public relations.

The interview went well and I joined Belk to generate publicity for the 15 to 20 new stores that the company was opening each year during the early 1980s. Several months later, I was named manager of the communications department and began supervising company publications, assisting John Belk and Tom Belk with speech writing, and handling other corporate communications.

It has been a privilege to serve in a position that has allowed me to work with two generations of Belk family leadership—first with John Belk and Tom Belk. Subsequently I worked with Tom's sons, Tim Belk, McKay Belk, and Johnny Belk, who are the company's chief executive officers today. Few family-owned companies survive past the second generation, yet Belk has defied the odds and is going strong nearly 120 years after William Henry Belk opened his first store in Monroe, North Carolina. It's one of the most remarkable and interesting stories in American business and free enterprise.

During my tenure, I've witnessed and been part of an extraordinary business transformation under the vision and direction of the Belk family. The company has evolved from a complex de-centralized organization composed of hundreds of separate store corporations and numerous operating units into a streamlined, highly-focused growth company that operates more than 300 leading fashion department stores throughout the South.

John and Tom Belk worked together at the helm of the company for nearly five decades. They built a strong foundation upon which the next generation of Belk leaders could expand and leverage the success of the company. The unexpected death of Tom Belk in January 1997 was a tragic shock to the company and to all who knew him. It was especially difficult for John Belk, who relied upon his brother as a business partner, confidante, and friend.

John moved quickly and strategically to transition the family leadership to the next generation and to establish a strong unified structure for the company that would enable it to be a strong and financially successful competitor for the long term. He continued to work closely with his nephews and other associates throughout the company until his retirement as chairman and CEO in 2004, just three years prior to his own untimely death on August 17, 2007, at age 87.

I was honored that Tony Zeiss asked me to contribute to this book about the wit and wisdom of John Belk and I applaud Tony for preparing this inspiring tribute to him. John was an extraordinary business and civic leader and philanthropist who, in spite of his frequent malapropisms, non sequiturs, and "Belkisms," communicated powerfully and effectively through his strong character, personality, and good humor.

John seemed to be larger than life. He was someone who was always on the forefront of his company and community, always working to make things better than when he first found them. He made a tremendous positive difference in the lives of thousands of people whom he touched through his roles as businessman, industry leader, public servant, philanthropist, family man, Boy Scout, sportsman, and many would add, comedian.

Here are some of the things that I remember most about John Belk:

He was a man of boundless energy and optimism with a strong work ethic instilled in him by his parents. He was always on the move and looking forward—you had to run to keep up with him whether at work or play.

He was a large man, both in physique and intellectual stature—the scope of his knowledge and influence was far-reaching. He was regarded as one of Charlotte's most powerful business and civic leaders who leveraged his clout to produce transformational change, progress, and success for his company and community.

He was highly charismatic. You could feel his presence when he entered the room. He had a trademark smile and sharp blue eyes that had a distinctive twinkle when he imparted his words of wit or wisdom.

He spoke a language all of his own, yet he always seemed to get his messages across. John was in constant demand as a speaker for management, stockholders, community and business groups and his "Belkese" and self-deprecating humor endeared him to others. During his tenure as mayor of Charlotte, reporters covering the government beat recorded many of his sayings, which became legendary.

He was humble and self-effacing in spite of his position of considerable power and wealth. In an interview for a video shown at his retirement dinner at Quail Hollow Club in May 2004, he said, "The more that you do for mankind the better you'll like life. Whether it's a company or city or state, you've got to leave it better for the next people coming along. You're just here for a short period of time."

He loved the City of Charlotte and was devoted to making it a better place to live, work, and play during his years of leadership with the Chamber of Commerce and as mayor. He was proud of his success in forging strong relationships between business and government to enable common goals and good plans for achieving progress and growth.

He worked with the news media on his own terms, sometimes leaving reporters befuddled and confounded by his quips and responses to questions that sometimes were beyond their understanding.

He was a consummate sportsman who treasured his experiences as a competitive athlete during his high school and college years, even playing against N.C. State's Bones McKinney while serving as captain of the Davidson College basketball team. He also loved collegiate and professional sports and enjoyed playing golf with some of the sport's greatest. He was particularly proud of being a partner with Jerry Richardson in the NFL Carolina Panthers football team.

He was a world traveler who reveled in learning all he could about the history and peoples of the far-flung places he visited, including Russia, Iceland, China and countries throughout Europe.

He believed in treating people with respect and cared deeply about Belk associates. He always made an extra effort to recognize and speak with employees during his frequent store visits and in the course of his day-to-day activities at the corporate office.

He loved to discuss politics, sports, and history and visits to his office often resulted in long lessons on local or world history, the latest sports developments, or reminiscing about his time spent at Davidson College.

He continued his father's rich legacy of community service and philanthropy through his leadership in and contributions to many worthy organizations and causes, and in particular to Davidson College, the Boy Scouts, the University of North Carolina at Charlotte, Central Piedmont Community College, and the Presbyterian Church.

He was devoted to his wife, Claudia, their daughter, Mary Claudia Pilon, and his three grandchildren.

Communicating John Belk's death was one of the most difficult and heart-wrenching experiences of my career at Belk. It was a sad day filled with a flood of emotions as I handled news media calls and worked with members of the Belk family and company executives to make announcements to employees, stockholders, and vendors and to prepare John's obituary and a memorial notice for *The Charlotte Observer*.

There was no time to grieve over the loss of a friend and legendary figure in my life and the lives of his family members and countless friends and associates. That would have to come later. And I suppose I'm still in denial. I somehow thought that John would always be around, that I would see him again bounding down the hallway or across the parking lot with a broad smile on his face and a twinkling in his blue eyes heading to his next meeting, golf outing, or home to his family.

John was an extraordinary man who lived life to the fullest and left a legacy of accomplishment and goodwill that will forever be remembered by those who knew and loved him. He truly left the world a better place as a result of his leadership and actions, and all of us are the beneficiaries. I thank God for John Belk and pray for God's continued blessings to his family, friends, and company.

Chapter One

Memories from Family and Friends

This chapter is designed to provide insight into John Belk's character as a boy, a Boy Scout leader, a military officer, a businessman, a governmental leader, a husband, a father, and a friend. This collection of stories is only a sample of those that will continue in the memories of the people who were so privileged to know him. Enjoy!

Shared by Claudia Belk, John's wife of thirty-six years, 1971-2007:

John used to refer to me affectionately as his "Sweet ole girl."

He loved American history and would often tell me and others how the Spanish brought gunpowder, horses, and priests to America, but the British brought law and order and leadership.

❃ ❃ ❃

John and his mother, Mary, loved each other but she didn't want him to box and he would sneak out to fight in the ring anyway. That's how he lost a tooth. They called him "Battling Belk."

Mary liked to watch him play basketball, but not when the playing got too rough. During one game when Davidson College was playing Chapel Hill, John was evidently playing very competitively because Mary told a preacher friend to tell John he was playing too rough and he was an embarrassment to the family. A few days later John told her that she didn't know anything about basketball if she thought he was too rough. "Besides," he explained, "I was being attacked by those two brothers who played for Carolina." She ignored the excuse and replied that she knew a lot about basketball because she played it when she was a girl.

❃ ❃ ❃

John and I used to spar over the proper spelling of our family name. John's mother's maiden name was Mary Lenora Irwin. Her ancestor was a General in the Revolutionary War. My name is Claudia Erwin (Watkins) Belk. John would often tell me that my family didn't know how to properly spell Irwin.

He would also tease me every time we drove to Charlotte Country Day School. They named a building there the Claudia Watkins Belk Hall. John would inevitably ask, "Who is Hall?"

I was serving as a district court judge when John and I married in 1971. He delighted in telling people that he married me and I gave him a life sentence.

❊ ❊ ❊

John, like most Southern people of his generation, would seldom complain directly about anything in public. He preferred to talk around the issue thereby avoiding being impolite. Not long ago, we were eating dinner at a new restaurant in SouthPark. The service was good, the atmosphere was good, and my meal was good, but John called the waiter over and told him he needed a sharp knife.

"Sir, you have a knife," the waiter replied.

"But I need a sharp one," John said. A short while later, the manager came over and asked John if he was having a problem with his knife. "Yes, I need a sharp knife," John repeated. They brought him another knife, but never understood that John was telling them that his duck was too tough.

❊ ❊ ❊

A reporter once asked John what he was going to do when he retired as mayor. "I'm going to read the Bible and learn to play the guitar!" He read the Bible, but never learned to play the guitar.

Shared by Mary Claudia (Belk) Pilon, John and Claudia's daughter:

My father never met a stranger and he loved people. No matter where he was, he always talked to people and made them feel comfortable.

As his daughter he made me feel comfortable with myself. I always knew he loved me because of his affection. As a child he sent me birthday cards even though we lived in the same house. He never signed them though. I guess he thought he could reuse them!

❦ ❦ ❦

When I was growing up, Dad would always get up early on weekends to spend time with me. He loved athletics and reading the newspaper. We would go swimming, play some sports, or sometimes just go for a walk. Sunday mornings were delightful. We would get up early and buy six dozen Krispy Kreme doughnuts and take them to his Sunday school class at Myers Park Presbyterian. Once when we were making the coffee prior to the arrival of his classmates, the huge coffee maker spewed all over the counter and flowed down and over the floor. Undaunted, Dad rushed to his automobile and brought back his golf towels to clean up the mess. I thought he was pretty smart in a crisis situation.

When I was homecoming queen at Charlotte Country Day School, Dad was across the country somewhere on business, but he sent flowers and a telegram. He asked my cousin Johnny Belk to stand in for him at the ceremony.

❦ ❦ ❦

There is one humorous event that I will never forget. The father-in-law of dad's long-time friend, Rail Brinson, had died and we went to the funeral and grave site memorial. Dad and Rail were pall bearers. It was wet and muddy from a recent rain and as they walked close to the open grave, Rail slipped and fell in. There was some serious commotion and people directed their attention to the grave when Rail came crawling out with Dad's help. He was covered with mud from head to toe. His wife exclaimed, "We don't know who that man is . . . never seen him before!"

I only saw my father cry four times. He cried at Rail Brinson's funeral, at his brother Tom's funeral, when he dropped me off on my first day of kindergarten, and when he dropped me off on my first day at Roanoke College.

When I was attending Roanoke College he always sent great letters and cartoons he'd clipped from the newspaper. This was his way of encouraging me and letting me know he was there if I needed him.

Dad loved history and believed we should all learn from it. That's where I gained an appreciation for it. He also loved his country and community and taught me that it is our responsibility to always give back.

Editor's Note: Mary Claudia and her husband, Jeff, are raising three children, James, Jack, and Katie. Mary Claudia is an active member of the May 20th Society and a leader in the Spirit of Mecklenburg project to build a statue to honor Captain James Jack of the Revolutionary War.

Shared by Sarah Belk Gambrell, John's sister:

My brother John loved to tease people, especially children. You can imagine my shock when I first saw John holding my very young daughter Sally over the balcony banister. She was only about three years old and I walked into the front room of Mother's house on Hawthorne Lane to see John holding Sally upside down by one ankle over the balcony. She was squealing with delight, but it frightened me to death!

Shared by Katherine "Kat" Belk, John's sister-in-law:

John and my husband Tom were always very close brothers. We spent a lot of time together before and after John married Claudia. During his bachelor days, John would sometimes bring a date along for whatever event or activity we were attending.

On one occasion, John brought a lady from New York to Aspen for a skiing trip we planned together. This woman had never been skiing so John explained it to her as best he could and rented her skis and boots. He showed her how to rest her skis on her shoulder for walking to the lift preparation area. She was doing well until she turned to look at something and the ski tips whacked John across his face. He sent her home!

Another time I invited a California friend to visit us in Charlotte. We introduced her to John and she stayed and stayed because she liked him. John took her to New York City for a visit and they took a carriage ride around Central Park. When they returned to the Plaza Hotel, they got into some kind of argument. John sent her back to California!

Tom and I were very grateful that Claudia came along!

John loved to cut up during family meals, especially at his mother's home where he lived during a good part of his bachelor days. He would start water fights with our children by flipping water across the table with his spoon. You'd have to wear a bathing suit to dinner!

His mother would have everyone over for Christmas dinner. She would sit at one end of the long table and John would sit at the other. She would generally ask John to return thanks. On one memorable occasion John bowed his head and prayed, "Dear Lord, we thank you for our sins." We were all shocked until we realized he meant to say, "We thank you for our blessings!"

Shared by Sally Gambrell Knight, John's niece:

We lived together in Grandmother's house for my first nine years of life, so Uncle John had plenty of time to play his mischief on me. Uncle John used to torture me at breakfast. He would put a teaspoon in the ice water and then flick the water across the table at me. No sooner would I retaliate than Grandma would look up and catch me in the act. Uncle John *never* got caught. His timing, of course, was perfect compared to a five-year-old girl. Still I kept trying.

That man would tease us to death and we loved him for it. He used to hold me upside down from high places and pretend to drop me. It took me many years to get the courage to ride in airplanes because I was afraid of heights, probably caused by Uncle John.

He also liked to wrap me in boxes at Christmas, and put my coats and toys on top of the grandfather clock. You never knew what he would do. It was fun and terrifying at the same time!

* * *

One of his favorite tricks was to steal one of my shoes and I would drive myself crazy trying to find it. I'd get all dressed up for church or school and couldn't find that second shoe. Then I would have to change outfits to match paired shoes. Years later, after Grandmother passed away, we found my six or eight single shoes behind the books in one bookshelf. John had dropped them there and never gave them back!

Shared by Tim Belk, John's nephew and chairman and CEO, Belk, Inc.:

Uncle John was a great friend and a wonderful mentor to my brothers, Johnny and McKay, our sister Katie and me. After my father died, Uncle John also became our surrogate father and treated my brothers and me as partners in the Belk department store business.

Uncle John's golf antics were legendary. My favorite one was the time John and two friends invited Louis Rose to Augusta National to play golf. Louis was understandably excited since serious golfers would give almost anything to play at the home of the Masters Tournament. It seems that the club was building a new bungalow near John's and it served a good purpose for John and his mischievous friends.

Upon arriving, John told Louis that there wasn't enough room in his place to accommodate four people, but there was an incomplete new bungalow which would be just fine for the fourth person. Since Louis was the newcomer, it would be his home for the evening. Louis was okay with the explanation and took his golf clubs and suitcase to the unfinished building. John and his friends watched with glee as Louis entered the bare-walled and concrete-floored bungalow. There was only one light bulb in the ceiling and the furniture consisted of an old U.S. Army cot and a makeshift bedside table.

Uncle John loved to recall the event describing how depressed his friend Louis appeared as he sat on the cot and slumped over in despair. Of course they all had a great laugh and Louis was moved into John's bungalow with the rest of the foursome.

Shared by Katie Belk Morris, John's niece:

I have many wonderful memories of John and I'm happy to share a few of those which are most notable to me.

Before John fell in love with Claudia, he was a big-time bachelor and had many glamorous girl friends. He spent a lot of free time over at our house in those days and with four small children it was usually chaotic, but lively. He loved that and would bring the girls over for dinner sometimes. It may have been a test of their character to see how they reacted to the bedlam. One time he brought a woman from California, which was an exotic place to us at that point. This woman had a child who was a TV star; he played Daniel Boone's son on a western show which we loved.

This celebrity was sent upstairs to play with us. We spent the night performing plays and finally did a magic trick with him where he disappeared in a drawer. He had a ball, but his mother did not approve at all. I remember Uncle John laughing and laughing at the trick. That was their last date. There were many girls who were after him, but he never seemed to pay them too much attention until Claudia came along. She was different, played hard to get, was smart, and had her own interests. He liked that.

I am also reminded that he was always curious, interested in new things, willing to learn and listen to anyone. At the same time, sometimes he did not hear what you said to him. When Jeff Pilon went up to the Belk corporate office to ask for permission to marry Mary Claudia, John was very tender. John thought Jeff said, "We want to get married on Friday," (it was Tuesday) and he immediately called Claudia to announce that Mary Claudia and Jeff were getting married on Friday. Claudia quickly called Jeff who said, "No, on Friday I am going to ask Mary Claudia if she will marry me. If she says yes, then we will set a date."

John loved my dad and loved all of my family as a result. I always felt that my mother was one of his favorite people also. He treated us as his children, especially after my dad died. I think he was very proud of my brothers and really enjoyed watching them develop as business people. He pushed them, but opened a lot of doors for them. He took pleasure in giving advice and introducing them to people he knew. We were all fortunate and blessed to be a part of his family.

Shared by Meb Wentz, John's God-daughter:

(Meb is the daughter of the late Robert Laurie Brinson, nicknamed "Rail" who met John at Davidson College, and became his life-long friend.)

When we were young, John would take all four of us children and sit us on top of the refrigerator and leave the room! He would then walk to the front door and open and shut it making us think he had left the house. I think he just loved to tease us or else he enjoyed hearing children scream.

When we visited John, I remember he always sat in a leopard recliner which he loved and he wore leopard pajamas! He also had a belt that was a tape measure that had the number "34" written on each inch line.

❖ ❖ ❖

Much of what I will always cherish about John Belk are the stories he and my father would tell about their younger days. John served in both World War II and in the Korean War. On one occasion Dad was home and told John that he would soon be shipping out again.

"Well, good luck," John offered.

Dad asked, "Don't you want to know where I'm going?"

"Sure," John replied.

"I'm shipping out to Charlotte in charge of the WACs," my dad reported. John thought it was so funny that my dad was coming to Charlotte and that he would be introducing John to all the pretty WACs.

❋ ❋ ❋

My favorite story was one they would talk about almost every time they were together. World War II was over and my father and John, both bachelors, decided they would take some rest and relaxation in a very popular Acapulco resort. All the Hollywood stars went there. John and Dad both had dates and were having a libation at a table next to the swimming pool when Errol Flynn walked up. They invited Flynn to join them and proceeded to enjoy several more drinks. All was going well until Flynn began to flirt with John's date. Finally, John got tired of Flynn's encroachment and threatened to run him off. I understand that John had been an avid boxer when he was younger.

No one quite remembered who threw the first punch, but John and Errol went at it. John must have been taking the worst of it because Dad entered the fight. It wasn't long until all three of them ended up in the swimming pool. They found out later that Errol Flynn had been a Golden Gloves Boxing champion before his Hollywood days. For the rest of their lives they would boast about beating "that Golden Glove champ."

Another John and Rail dating story is worth sharing. Young Rail and John were in Miami once and they got connected with blind dates. They had such a good time the two Romeos cancelled their flights back to Charlotte so they could date the ladies again the next night. That airplane crashed on its way back to Charlotte and it had no survivors. John and Dad always said, "Pretty women saved their lives."

❋ ❋ ❋

John's father, William Henry, died while John was serving in the Korean War. John got a furlough, but it took several weeks for him to arrive home.

My father said, "John, it must be very hard for you to lose your father."

"Yes, Rail," John replied, "but life is for the living."

John and my father were such good friends; John even went with him and my mother on their honeymoon! John was still single and I don't know how that worked out, but they remained friends to the end.

Dad often related the incident about how he and John attended the funeral of another good friend, Haskell Porcher. They were attending Haskell's grave site memorial when a nearby train rattled through with its horn blowing. The preacher stopped talking and everyone just had to endure it until the train and its noise passed. Before the preacher could begin again, John quipped, "There goes Haskell, he's moving on!"

When Rail and John were deep in their seventies or early eighties, they played at a golf tournament at Grandfather Golf and Country Club near Linville. They had won their flight even though John had just had a hip replacement and Dad was recovering from eye surgery.

Later that evening, my brother-in-law, Hank Cunningham, was visiting with two young friends in Greensboro. He asked how they were doing at their golf game.

"Just terrible," they replied. "We were just beaten in a golf tournament by an old cripple and a blind man!"

❖ ❖ ❖

My parents traveled with John and Claudia to Mary Claudia's graduation from Roanoke College. They all had a meal at a five-star restaurant in Roanoke. Upon receiving the bill, John asked to see the manager. The manager came over to their table and asked how he could be of assistance. John replied, "I only wanted to pay the bill for the food, not buy the restaurant!"

At another restaurant one time, John handed the waiter a credit card to pay for the meal. In a few minutes, the waiter returned and announced that the card had expired. John explained, "It was good when we came in here. If it hadn't taken so long to get our meals, it would still be good!"

One time at the Charlotte Country Club, the waitress picked up John's plate when it was still half full. As the young waitress lifted his plate, John exclaimed, "If I had known you were so hungry, I would have left you a full plate!"

❆ ❆ ❆

Just a few years ago my husband, Russ, went with John to see the new movie *Gods and Generals* produced by Ted Turner. Afterward, John raved about the movie and said Ted Turner was brilliant because he ended the movie with the South still winning!

John Belk always wanted folks to look at the positive side of things. One time at a Panther's game we were all in the Belk suite and the Panthers were losing terribly. Everyone was depressed until John spoke up. "Look at the cheerleaders. Aren't they fantastic? See what happens when you work as a team!"

Shared by Nancy Williams, John's first cousin:

My father was Henderson Irwin, John's uncle and brother to John's mother. Whenever they would visit us at our home he would always tease me by saying, "Hello Nancy purple, yellow, blue, orange, or green," playing off my name which was Nancy Lavender Irwin. He loved to tease.

At dinner time at the Belk home, John would sit by the biscuits. Whenever someone would ask to have the biscuits passed, John would throw one to him or her at the other end of the table. This was a trademark antic at any dinner when Aunt Mary was entertaining a large group. Of course, John knew she would be quite embarrassed!

On one occasion, young John decided to see if he could hit one of my father's ducks with a corn cob. He threw the cob and hit the duck squarely on the head. It was an instant death for the duck. John worried about it all day long and finally told my father while we were having dinner. He was thanked for telling the truth. After that, John always said he killed Uncle Hen's prize duck!

* * *

Once, when my husband, Charlie, and our two daughters visited Aunt Mary's home in Charlotte, John began chasing our daughters Nancy Anne and Mary Katherine and his niece, Sally Gambrell, all over the house. After catching all three, he promptly put them in the shower with their clothes on and turned on the water! It was great fun for all.

I vividly remember all five of those Belk boys getting into a fracas over some issue or another and they would end up in a heap on the floor. Aunt Mary, their mother, would get a switch and start swatting them until they quit wrestling. All five of those boys went on to fight in World War II. Thankfully, all five returned home safely.

After returning from Korea, John lived with his mother Mary (Irwin) Belk at their home on Hawthorne Lane in Charlotte. He loved leading his Boy Scout troop and would often invite all of his scouts over for lunch or dinner and requested menus that would appeal to his boys. I was attending Queens College at the time and Aunt Mary always invited me to these dinners to help her serve all those hungry scouts. John took his responsibility as a scout leader very seriously and truly enjoyed "his boys."

Shared by Leroy Robinson, former executive for Belk Stores Services:

John Belk was the best friend I ever had. He meant so much to our community, the Belk stores, and to everyone he met.

John's mind usually worked faster than his ability to speak and he would often confuse people. But on this occasion, John was perfectly clear in mind and speech. This incident has been talked about for decades and will no doubt continue to be talked about for years to come.

When John was mayor of Charlotte, one citizen who was opposed to the airport expansion asked John why the airport was put on the west side of town in the first place. In typical Belk fashion, John replied, "Because that's where the airplanes land."

This community and those who knew him miss him deeply.

Shared by Carrie Robinson, John's housekeeper for 37 years:

I can truly say it has been wonderful working here for 37 years. I've met so many top-level people and friends of the family.

Mr. Belk, while mayor, threw the first pitch for my son's little league baseball team in 1974. He was a loyal man to what he cared about and he was a die-hard fan of the Panthers. He loved sports and never missed a Panthers game unless he was out of town.

He was a devoted husband, a caring father and grandfather, and he was full of life and laughter. He also enjoyed traveling and reading. He loved his younger brother, Tom. When Tom died, it was a big loss for Mr. Belk. I guess we shared the pain since I lost a sister the same week.

Every morning you were always greeted with a "Good morning!" and with a nice sense of humor. Mr. Belk generally had a bowl of cereal with fruit and a cup of coffee. He would sit in his favorite chair and read the newspaper and maybe a magazine before leaving for work.

He had a very sharp memory and could take you way back remembering the exact dates of events. He was a fine conversationalist, especially after a Panther's game. He made it possible for my family and me to attend all the Panther games with tickets and parking passes. We really appreciated that!

There is no way to adequately sum up what Mr. Belk meant to the city of Charlotte. The love he had for his friends and family was overwhelming. His personality touched everyone he met and he will be remembered for his kindness, his jokes, his unique way with words, and his devotion to his family and his church.

He is greatly missed and will always be in our hearts. I am very grateful for the friend I found in him.

Shared by Colonel Terry Vangen, John's commanding officer in Korea:

John was called into active duty by the U.S. Army during the Korean War and went to Korea as an officer of the United Nations Civil Assistance Command. I was in command of the United Nations' troops in and around the Eighth Army Headquarters. I remember John as a Second Lieutenant and later, upon my recommendation, as a First Lieutenant. John later became Captain of his company. He was assigned to help create small businesses and to assist the local citizens cope with the ravages of war. He was successful in developing some rice factories and getting some that had been damaged by bombs back into operation.

John was gregarious, ambitious, and a good athlete. He was an excellent volleyball player and could pitch horseshoes with the best of them. He was very civic minded and had high integrity. He became friends with many Presbyterian missionaries, some of whom were physicians. Dr. Underwood and Dr. Crane were part of this ministry and John supported them both. He also founded a Boy Scout group.

My wife and I were privileged to visit John and Claudia on several occasions and thoroughly enjoyed it. They took us to a Panthers' game and to other activities in Charlotte.

Shared by Johnny Harris, long-time close friend, and CEO of Lincoln-Harris, LLC:

Even if John disagreed with you, he'd stand by you, but he would never let you forget it! John and I attended a Charlotte Chamber intercity visit to Dallas. At that time, I was leading a construction bond referendum for a new National Basketball Association coliseum. John thought the arena should be placed downtown and my colleagues and I thought it belonged on the edge of town. At one point during our intercity visit, John chewed me out in front of all the participants and told me in no uncertain terms what he thought about the placement of the coliseum.

After John left the room, chamber leaders apologized to me and were surprised at Mr. Belk's scolding. Later that afternoon I ran into John at the Anatole Hotel where he was obviously waiting for me. He asked me to have a drink with him and I did. Although he never mentioned the chastisement, it was his way of demonstrating that although he disagreed with me, it wouldn't get in the way of our friendship.

❊ ❊ ❊

John was famous for his jokes and stories. He had an excellent memory and often used his jokes and anecdotes to make a point. Sometimes, he would bungle up the joke or the story, but would land on his feet every time.

On most days, John's assistant, Debra Byers, would type up two jokes on note cards and he would put them in his pocket for use at the proper time that day. At one community leadership event, John was speaking and he pulled out a card and told the joke. Just before delivering the punch line, he turned over the card and read the wrong punch line. The audience was stunned into silence. Stuart Dickson and I began laughing because we recognized what he had done and pretty soon all of his close friends were roaring with laughter at the situation, but everyone else was confused.

❊ ❊ ❊

In 1989 John, Hugh McColl, Governor Jim Martin, Steve Camp, and I flew on a NationsBank airplane to Traverse City, Michigan, to make a pitch to the National Collegiate Athletic Association. We wanted a tournament in Charlotte. We had rehearsed many times and everyone knew what he was going to say.

Our presentation was to follow Governor Cuomo and Bill Bradley from New York City. John was the first speaker and he immediately got off his script. He addressed these officials by stating, "This sort of reminds me of the Red Cap porter at the old Charlotte railroad station."

When asked what his average tip was, the porter replied, "It is five dollars."

"That's your average tip?" he was asked.

"No, most people don't give me an average tip!"

John then sat down. We all sat in nervous silence until someone finally laughed. It made no sense to us. Later John explained that he just wanted to break the ice.

That was John Belk—unpretentious and unpredictable.

Shared by Bishop George Battle, lifetime friend of John Belk:

Few people have had as much influence on my development as John Belk. When I was eighteen years old I walked into the Rock Hill Belk store and met Mr. Farrow, the store manager. I asked him if he needed someone to run the store's elevator. He asked if I knew how to operate it. I replied that I did not, but that I could learn. Mr. Farrow hired me and helped me in many ways including sharing his lunch each day. He would eat at the local Elks Club and bring half his lunch back to the store for me.

Mr. Farrow had a tendency to snooze standing up and Mr. John Belk had the unsettling habit of visiting stores when he was least expected. One lazy afternoon Mr. Farrow was snoozing with his head down and his arms crossed when Mr. Belk walked in. As he approached Mr. Farrow the floor must have creaked because Mr. Farrow opened his eyes, saw John's big shoes, and quickly vocalized an "Amen." He then greeted Mr. Belk.

Mr. Belk said, "Mr. Farrow, there will always be a job here for reverent men!"

※ ※ ※

Back then, people smoked everywhere, even in the store. They would carelessly burn holes in shirts, pants, and sweaters. Of course we couldn't sell damaged goods and I was given all the damaged clothes I needed. They said I was the best dressed man at Livingstone College. I once overheard John and Mr. Farrow discussing the damaged clothes situation and John said to Mr. Farrow, "I wish they smoked with the lighted end inside their mouths so we would lose fewer clothes!"

I later came to be the first black person to sell clothes on the floor and became their number one sales person in the men's section. They wanted me to work full time with them, but I had already chosen the ministry for my career. I attended Livingstone College and was ready for the commencement, but found that I owed $250 to the college and would not be allowed to walk in the commencement ceremonies unless the debt was paid. On the very day of commencement I received a $250 check from John as a graduation gift and was able to march in my commencement.

Shared by Susan Jetton, a former *Charlotte Observer* reporter:

My first impression was that this new mayor couldn't talk. I learned that you had to listen closely before you could begin to understand him. He will always be Charlotte's mayor to me. He was dumb like a fox and had a wonderful heart.

He was a really good mayor. I never knew anyone who loved this city more than Mr. Belk. He was fond of saying, "I'm mighty proud of the fine city of Charlotte!" This was his main tag line. I can still see him in the mayor's office holding up the telephone cord while the receiver spun around and around to unwind.

✳ ✳ ✳

John once hosted several mayors from around the state. They played golf and a lunch was prepared for them and us reporters. The big event was to be held at the Quail Hollow Country Club and I arrived in time to follow a male reporter to the luncheon location. I followed him straight into the men's locker room! I was told I had to leave since no women could be allowed into the men's locker room. John heard about my expulsion and made the staff take down the tables and reset them upstairs in the dining room so I could also attend.

I think Claudia coined the term "Belkese" whenever someone had trouble understanding John. Wylie Williams, then an assistant city manager, explained the mayor's Belkese by stating that "John's mind ran at 45 RPMs and his mouth only ran at 33 ⅓."

John absolutely worshipped Claudia from the time they began dating through the rest of his life. He was very excited about marrying her and no man has ever been more excited about his wife's pregnancy. He was once asked what they would name the baby.

"Why, Mary Claudia, what else?" John replied.

※ ※ ※

John had a wonderful way of diffusing tension in city council meetings. He would often interject something that at first sounded strange or odd, but would end up diverting people from their concerns. Humor was his best weapon on these occasions. He could also give a sharp rebuke when one was needed. He once told a contentious citizen, "You are educated beyond your knowledge!"

John Belk was a courtly gentleman, often making comments about sitting between the pillars of two Ruths—city clerk Ruth Armstrong and city council member Ruth Easterling. Ruth Easterling was appointed to fill a vacancy on city council. It had been a bitter process and was perceived to have been done behind closed doors. I had an inside source who was party to all of it and I wrote about all the machinations of the behind-the-scene activities.

On the Monday after the Sunday story ran, we all went on a tour of a construction site before the council meeting that evening. I was reluctant to go because I knew several members would be critical of me and my story. Sure enough, they began criticizing me right away until Mayor Belk walked up and said, "Susan, I didn't know you had begun to write fiction!" That diffused the situation and we all laughed.

※ ※ ※

I left Charlotte for a number of years, but every time John saw me in later years he would say, "Isn't this just what we planned? I told you this is what would happen. Just look at the inner belt, the outer belt, and the airport."

Shared by Belinda Crowell, John's assistant while he was mayor of Charlotte:

John was a real people person. He enjoyed making personal connections with people from all walks of life. He was a serious business man, but there was a soft side to him. We always called each other on our birthdays. He continued to call me on my birthday after he was mayor until his death. It pleased me that a man of his stature and importance thought enough of me to do this. He also attended my daughter's wedding in 2002.

While I was working with John, my parents owned a store two miles from Myrtle Beach. He owned the Saint John's Inn also at Myrtle Beach. Once while he was staying at his hotel, John took the time to visit my parents at their store.

From that point forward he always introduced me by saying, "This is Belinda, and she's her mother's apple."

Shared by Frances Killian Hampton, John's secretary from 1946-1955
(As published in *The Charlotte Observer*, September 9, 2007)**:**

John Belk became my boss in 1946 shortly after his return from World War II. For the next nine years, excepting his Army service in Korea, I worked as his personal secretary.

John was the kindest person I ever knew. One day I looked out my office window on East Fifth Street and saw him sitting at the railroad crossing, bandaging a young black boy's foot. John was on his way to see George Dowdy, manager of the uptown Belk store, but his meeting had to wait. John never knew I saw him that day, nor did I ever tell him.

Shared by Debra Byers, John's assistant at Belk Stores Services for many years:

John Belk was delightful to work for and it was a privilege to get to know him so well. He was all business, but had a delightful sense of humor and cared about people, especially his family, friends, employees, and anyone who lived in Charlotte.

Mr. Belk's driving reputation was notorious. We called his Lincoln the 'Silver Bullet' because he drove so fast. When he would get into a fender bender, which was frequent, I had to take care of insurance, car repairs, and whatever else was required. He never told me when he had a new collision so I established the habit of walking around his car about every other day to see if there was any new damage. When I found evidence of some new accident I would ask him how it happened and he'd always respond, "Claudia did it!" Of course Claudia never drove his cars.

Claudia told me that once when they had rented a car in Los Angeles and were driving to Palm Springs, John ran over something and it was dragging underneath the car. She asked John what he had hit. John told her he didn't know and kept driving. After several miles whatever it was let loose.

❖ ❖ ❖

One morning Mr. Belk asked me to drive him and Leroy Robinson from our corporate office to SouthPark. When we got to Tyvola and South Boulevard John quipped, "I could have done had us there." I ignored the remark and kept driving.

At the next turn, Leroy said, "Well, Debra, I would have turned back there." I refused to drive them after that.

Another time I tried to follow Mr. Belk from the Charlotte Country Club back to our corporate offices, but he drove so fast, I lost him in the first three blocks.

❋ ❋ ❋

Editor's Note: One Saturday afternoon in 2006 my wife, Beth, and I were driving out West Boulevard when a big Lincoln flew by us.

"Who is that crazy guy?" I exclaimed.

"Mercy, that's John Belk!" Beth replied.

That incident confirmed one of John's favorite sayings that he had no problem with Charlotte traffic, except for those people who got in his way!

Shared by Susan Jamison, John's long-time financial advisor:

I worked with John for fifteen years as his financial advisor. He seldom thought women were the best for a job, but if he selected a woman for a job, you knew he thought highly of her.

He often said he made his contribution to society when he married Claudia and removed a female judge from the workforce. He was teasing, of course.

John would have been the same caring person whether he had money or not. He loved people and life. He saw his money as a blessing. He believed the scripture, "Unto much is given, much is expected." He was very generous with his money and loved to support good causes.

Thirty years from now I will always remember that we had fun. He had a wonderful little grin and a twinkle in his eye when you did something well.

Shared by Carol M. Cannon, John's administrative assistant from 1956 to 1989:

Mr. Belk was a remarkable person with a wonderful personality, who never met a stranger. Many people said they felt that I knew him better than anyone else, but that's not true. Just when I thought I had him figured out, he would change a bit!

* * *

One time when John went to Jacksonville to visit friends, he asked my assistant to see that his golf clubs and luggage were checked in at the airport ahead of time. The person who took his golf clubs to the airport found two sets of clubs in the trunk. Not knowing which to send, he sent both sets! When John landed in Jacksonville and recovered his luggage, he discovered he had two set of clubs! He called me immediately and asked what he was supposed to do with two sets of golf clubs! I asked, "Do you think two sets of clubs will help you play a better game?"

There was dead silence on the phone, so I knew he failed to see the humor in the situation. I apologized and suggested that he get a porter to help him put one set in a locker.

* * *

Everyone knew you couldn't get in the last word with John Belk, and shouldn't even try, without paying for it later!

My daughter worked for NationsBank and often dropped by my office on the way home, to say hello to Mr. Belk if he was there. She had a great admiration for him and he liked to tease her. John had just returned to the office from playing golf one day and was wearing bright red trousers.

"How are things at the bank?" he asked of her.

"Just fine," she replied, "but I see you're in the red today!"

He grinned at her and walked into his office. That is the only time I ever saw him wordless, without a comeback!

❦ ❦ ❦

When John Belk became mayor of Charlotte, he discovered there was no secretary provided and he would have to share the city manager's secretary. He then said to me, "When we go to city hall . . ." But I interrupted him to say, "You are going to City Hall, but I'm staying here!"

Later a secretary was hired to serve just the mayor, and I continued as his assistant at Belk. His secretary at city hall and I talked every day to keep his schedule straight and up to date. He was so busy with both responsibilities that I devised a card that would fit into his shirt pocket that listed his appointments and obligations for each day. He continued to use that card system during the years after he was mayor.

❦ ❦ ❦

John Belk loved Charlotte, North Carolina, and America! He was the best ambassador to the rest of the country (and other countries) that Charlotte ever had. He said Charlotte had been good to him, and he wanted to give back. He was a generous, kind, sincere, and thoughtful person.

Shared by Paulette Purgason, who served on the city manager's staff when John was mayor:

I first met John when I was in my twenties and working with Stan Brookshire who was serving as mayor. I would often go up Trade Street to the Belk headquarters and have lunch at their lunch counter. It was a long room that ran the length of the building, much like a long soda fountain. John was standing at the steps going up to the lunch room one day just after announcing he was a candidate for mayor.

When I started up the steps, he grabbed my hand and started shaking it. "Hello, there. My, what big brown eyes you have. I'm John Belk."

I told him my name.

He replied, "Then you must be the young woman Mayor Brookshire told me about."

I answered with something like, "Oh, then you may be my new boss."

He said, "Probably, since the other guy will lose!" He was always confident.

* * *

No one was too small or insignificant to get John's attention. He remembered names and many of them probably got birthday cards from him. He'd often tell me and other staff members to go down to Belk and pick something nice for our birthdays. He was a true Southern gentleman who cared about people and Charlotte. I don't think most people fully understand all that he did for them and our community.

I served him during all four terms he was mayor and he introduced the world to me. It was an honor to serve "His Honor," and also during his tenure as chairman of the Airport Advisory Authority. By this time I was the Airport Communications specialist. He wore plaid pants that were too short and a coat to match, but that was before Claudia came along.

Shared by Mason Wallace, a high school and college pal and lifetime friend:

I first met John at the McCallie School in Chattanooga, Tennessee, in 1935 or 1936. It was a fine college prep school for boys. We both attended there because they had cut back public schools in Charlotte to only seven months a year because of a shortage of funds. John first attended Central High School in Charlotte. We later attended Davidson College together and joined the same fraternity, Kappa Alpha. We were great friends from the beginning. John's nickname was Long John and mine was Moose.

Another fraternity brother was Charlie Watt. He later became a well-respected surgeon. Charlie was a very serious student and that's why

John liked to tease him. Charlie also loved reading the sports pages in the Charlotte newspaper. He would sit in a chair, cross his legs, and become completely engrossed in the sports stories, oblivious to anything else around him. John liked to pour rubbing alcohol on his extended shoe and set it on fire. I can still see those blue flames as they caught the newspaper on fire and smoke swirled around ole Charlie. After a time or two of this, Charlie would lock himself in his room when reading the newspaper. Undaunted, John would lay a piece of the paper on the floor, drip some alcohol on it, light it up, and slip it under Charlie's door.

One of the best nights of entertainment in my life was with John Belk. We decided to visit Manhattan and have some fun so we cranked up that Plymouth of his, drove to New York City, and picked up two dates in mid-town Manhattan. We went to Glen Island Casino, had a wonderful dinner, and heard Glenn Miller play. Later we went to a club and heard Count Basie! It was a memorable night!

John and I went off to World War II and lost track of each other for a while. I was a Lieutenant and was wounded three times. At Anzio I spotted a cherry tree that was full of fruit. We hadn't had any fruit in a year so up the tree I climbed. I got a few cherries and threw them to the boys before I fell out of the tree. Some others broke bones when they fell out, but nothing was hurt on me but my pride.

When I got back to Charlotte I was scheduled to get married. We were holding a luncheon at the Charlotte Country Club and we were to get married that evening. I told John that morning that I was ill and needed to go home and sleep. John called Dr. Bill Matthews and asked for his help. Dr. Matthews said it was his day off, but John insisted that he look at me and he came over. I made it to the lunch and the wedding. After that I always told John that he got me married and I had suffered ever since! John would reply by telling me she was the best thing that ever happened to me!

Shared by John McCaskill, a long-time Belk corporate administrator and friend of John:

John Belk was a great friend, boss, and mentor. He could motivate you with just one word. One year he was chair of the annual Charlotte Chamber membership drive for the Belk team. The first report that came out from the Chamber showed the Belk team at the bottom of the list. He sent it to me with one word beside our entry-why?-followed by his initials JMB. I can guarantee you we got serious about raising members.

John was a very generous man. On one occasion he offered my wife and me use of his condominium for the weekend. Sometime later out of the clear blue, John said, "I guess you didn't have a very good time at the condominium."

I was puzzled and asked him why he thought that.

"Well, you haven't asked if you could go back!"

Back in the eighties our SouthPark store was thoroughly remodeled and we decided to do a grand reopening. We put on an absolutely outstanding black tie event. We had the Junior League involved, we had orchestras on every floor, and food and drink stations were set up all over the store. Oscar de la Renta was there and hundreds of people attended. Needless to say, we were very proud of the event. The next morning, John listened to us compliment each other on how great the reopening was and how it was good public relations for the store.
John allowed us to go on for a while then stated, "It don't take a smart man to spend somebody else's money!" It humbled us all.

Nothing seemed to faze John or shake his confidence. For example, when I was chair of the annual Carrousel Parade on Thanksgiving Day here in Charlotte, I rode in a run-of-the-mill convertible. John, as mayor, and Claudia rode in a vintage Ford Roadster with a rumble seat. About a block or so into the parade, the Roadster broke down. John jumped out and hailed my car down and said, "How about a lift?" They rode the rest of the way with me and had as good a time as if they'd stayed in the Roadster.

Shared by Stuart Dickson, lifetime friend of John:

John was one of the most incredible people I ever met. His brother, Tom, and I were very close friends and I've known John for most of my life. We got really close after Tom passed away.

Neither John nor Tom could handle the King's English very well. However, if you learned "Belkese," you could understand them.

John also had a self-deprecating sense of humor that people loved. Senator Robert Pittenger brought Margaret Thatcher to town once and John and I attended. John was presiding and giving the introduction to the Prime Minister.

"Mrs. Thatcher," John began, "we started out in politics together. For you they said, here comes the Lord's mayor. For me they said, Lord, here comes the mayor!"

❉ ❉ ❉

When Dr. John Kuykendall became president of Davidson College in 1984, he made a passionate plea to the Executive Committee of the Board for his first budget. John and I were both members of this committee. This budget included a three and a half percent raise for the faculty. He really wanted to be able to give a raise to the faculty in his first year as president.

John listened to Dr. Kuykendall and then stated, "A hungry dog runs a long trail, but a fat pig will lie close to the barn." Dr. Kuykendall seemed confused and leaned over to me.

"What did he say? What did he say?" he asked.

I said, "He means okay, but if you overpay people, they'll become fat and lazy."

John Belk said, "That's exactly what I mean."

John never missed anything worthwhile and he and Claudia would often make three or four events in one evening. Often people would be astonished that he would attend their event exclaiming something like, "John, we didn't really expect you to come to this small gathering."

He would always reply, "Why are you surprised, you invited me didn't you?"

Claudia once said, "John, you must not have been invited to anything as a boy or young man because now you won't miss anything!"

❊ ❊ ❊

To wrap it up, no one has done more for Charlotte than John Belk. He served over eight years as mayor, held every major civic leadership position including leading the Charlotte Chamber and the Boy Scout Board. Under his leadership, Charlotte was launched to be the city it is today. Just consider his vision and influence regarding the airport, the highway loops, the revitalization of downtown, the Government Center, and the elimination of the depressed areas downtown. He will be missed.

Shared by Pat McCrory, current mayor of Charlotte:

John Belk has been one of my heroes even before I first ran for city council, but now that I've been mayor for all these years, I've come to respect him even more. He often pretended he didn't know as much as he did . . . it was an act. He was brilliant in a strategic way.

When I was mayor pro tem, I called John and asked to come and visit him explaining that I was thinking of running for mayor, but I needed his wisdom and advice. John and I belonged to opposite political parties, but I felt comfortable asking for his advice. John said he didn't know what was going on in Charlotte anymore, but I could come to visit if I wanted to. When I visited him a few days later he proceeded to tell me everything that was going on with the city, including things I wasn't aware of as mayor pro tem!

After I had been elected mayor, John came by to see me at the Government Center downtown. When he left he found that he had a parking ticket. He called me and I told him I was sorry, but I couldn't fix anybody's ticket. After all, he'd been the mayor and knew it could be political suicide to get involved in such shenanigans.

Two years later when I was running for reelection, I ran into John and out of the blue he asked, "Do you remember that parking ticket?"

I answered in the affirmative. John replied, "Good. Consider that as my contribution to your next campaign!"

"Fine," I replied, "that is about double what you gave me last time!"

I was told that when John was mayor he had a parking space at the airport. He would not tell me where he continued to park at the airport, and for years I asked him about it at every public opportunity. He never did tell me and he never stopped using it!

❖ ❖ ❖

Editor's Note: I have it on good authority that John only had a parking space for a short time and it was eliminated by new construction. After that, he always made his own space in front of the airport by parking where he pleased, whether there was a space or not!

Shared by Dottie Crowell, long-time friend of John:

John and my husband, Bob, were lifelong friends going back to their college days at Davidson. Years ago, John and Bob were competing in a golf tournament in Tampa, Florida, at the Palma Ceia Golf Club, noted for its tight fairways. John was prone to spray some shots out of the fairway and on one hole he found himself in the rough. While looking for his ball, he came upon another lost ball that was bright and shiny and not visibly marked except for the personalized imprint of *Leon Sikes*. Since Mr. Sikes, a well-known golfer from the area, was unknown to John and, according to others in their foursome, nowhere in sight, the ball quickly found its way into John's pocket. A few holes later John put the newly acquired ball into play. The third fairway at Palma Ceia parallels the ninth fairway and a slice from the tee box can easily land in the middle of the adjoining fairway, which is exactly where John's drive headed.

John strode toward a ball in the center of the ninth fairway, checked to see that it was labeled *Leon Sikes* and prepared to hit his next shot. As he addressed the ball, a golfer approached from the opposite direction. Before John hit, the other golfer called out, "Check that ball! I am sure it's my ball!"

John replied confidently, "I know it is my ball because it is clearly marked with the name *Leon Sikes*."

Imagine John's amazement and dismay when the approaching golfer called back, "Well, I am Leon Sikes!"

John relinquished rights to the ball, Leon continued playing the ninth hole, and John resumed the search for the other *Leon Sikes* ball.

Shared by Jim Babb, long-time friend of John:

The incident that I recall is one about him as a young man. John and several of his friends decided to raft down the Catawba River when it was restricted to do so. They evidently much enjoyed their escapade until they were arrested for breaking the law. They called John's parents and he was released into their custody! To my knowledge, this incident didn't make it into the news during any of his mayoral campaigns.

Shared by Luther Moore, Belk senior vice president and assistant general counsel:

John Belk was revered by his employees and they held him in the highest regard. One incident illustrates this environment very well.

John often visited his stores and once when he and Erskine Harkey were in South Carolina, John pumped his own gas and splashed it all over himself. They drove on and visited several stores even though John smelled like a gas station. Not one person he met with mentioned a thing about it.

John often asked me to sit in meetings he had with political candidates. Once he asked me to sit with him as he visited with a Congressional candidate. They visited for an hour and the candidate never asked John for a nickel. This was probably due to the fact that John would intentionally intimidate candidates to see how they handled it.

* * *

On another occasion, a different candidate for Congress visited John and they talked about history for an hour and a half and never talked much about his candidacy. He didn't get any money from John, though the candidate asked for some.

Of course people like Bishop George Battle could always get money out of John. John cared deeply about good people who wanted to help the people of Charlotte.

After hearing about all the special events planned to honor John upon his retirement, he commented, "If I'd known I was so important, I wouldn't have retired!"

Shared by Joan Zimmerman, long-time friend of John:

Once, while traveling with the airport authority to West Palm Beach, John had arranged for the authority members to meet and eat at the West Palm Beach Country Club. We walked into the club and the club manager pulled John aside, while looking at me, the only female in the group. It was obvious what was being said. It was even more obvious when John, not so quietly, said, "If Joan doesn't eat in here, none of us eat in here, and that means ever!" Of course we were seated.

I squirmed and later laughed a lot about the time John introduced Margaret Thatcher. It was a very special evening at Quail Hollow

Country Club and John introduced Lady Thatcher with a host of interesting stories. He then paused and said, "Lady Margaret Thatcher."

Thinking this was her cue to speak, she stood up.

John said, "I'm not finished yet, sit down." He continued his introduction and again paused and said, "Lady Margaret Thatcher," in a definitive tone. Once again, up she stood to approach the lectern. John repeated that he wasn't finished yet and would she please sit down. Finally, after three mis-starts, John said, "Okay, now it's time."

Mrs. Thatcher said, as only a British diplomat could, "Well! I don't know when I have had a more interesting introduction!"

Shared by Bob Dalton, high school chum and life-long friend:

Very few people ever ordered John Belk around, except his mother and father of course. But I witnessed just such an event one evening when Margaret Thatcher visited Charlotte at Robert Pittenger's invitation. It was a fine formal affair and John introduced Mrs. Thatcher and sat on the dais with her. After her address, she entertained questions from the audience. In his attempt to be a good host, John would jump up each time and announce who was asking the question. This gesture began to annoy Mrs. Thatcher who finally turned to John and said, "John, sit down and be quiet!" He sat down without a word.

❖ ❖ ❖

John and I attended the McCallie School in Chattanooga together. After high school, he went to Davidson College and I attended North Carolina State. On one occasion John and I decided to invite a coed group of our high school-aged friends to spend the weekend at the beach. My mother went along as the chaperone. We finally worked up the courage to ask her if we could smoke. She answered in the affirmative and one of our friends pulled out one of those thin wood-tipped Havana cigars and offered it to her as a joke. "Give me one of those," she requested. He gave her one and she smoked it! I guess she was broad minded in that way.

❦ ❦ ❦

John had an old Ford with no top and everyone used to love riding in it. One of John's fraternity brothers drove it in reverse from Davidson to Charlotte on a dare. We enjoyed that car and so did the girls!

Shared by Bob Rogers, former CEO of Texas Industries and a business friend of John:

I would like to share an event generally called "The Last Supper" that provides some insight into the workings of high-level business and corporate board intrigue. John Belk and Bill Lee, CEO of Duke Power, had been on the Board of Associates Corporation of North America for several years. They had urged Associates' President and CEO, Reece Overcash, to hold one of its quarterly directors' meetings in Charlotte. After all, Charlotte was fast becoming an important financial center and Associates was generating an enviable record of success in the few short years since it moved from Indiana to Dallas, Texas. A directors' meeting in Charlotte would provide good visibility for the company. Also, Reece Overcash knew and loved Charlotte and maintained a residence there. Reece agreed that the September 1986 directors' meeting would be held in the board room of the North Carolina National Bank, now Bank of America, with a reception and dinner to be held the previous evening at the Charlotte Country Club.

At this time, Associates was a wholly-owned subsidiary of Gulf and Western Industries and its CEO, Marty Davis, was a member of Associates' Board. He, of course, would attend the dinner and the directors' meeting in Charlotte. The limousine and driver scheduled to pick up Mr. Davis from the private air terminal at the Charlotte airport had been hired from an Atlanta firm. Unfortunately, the driver was unfamiliar with Charlotte. What was supposed to be a twenty-minute drive from the airport to the country club turned into an hour and twenty minutes of frustration, particularly for Marty Davis!

Marty was proud of his position as Gulf and Western's CEO and was not a man known for his patience. The evening festivities at the club were delightful. Charlotte civic leaders were in attendance and glowing praise flowed in support of the accomplishments of Associates Corporation and its leader, Reece Overcash. Not one word of acknowledgment was spoken, much less praise, for Marty Davis.

After the board meeting the next morning, Mr. Davis informed Reece Overcash that Associates no longer needed an outside Board of Directors. The lack of perspective shown at the previous evening's gathering was sufficient to convince Marty that a group of independent directors was unnecessary. When this news became known, some felt that Mr. Davis had taken the action because the quality of the outside directors on Associates' Board far exceeded that of its parent company, Gulf and Western. Others chalked the decision up to the egotism and temper of Marty Davis.

John Belk simply referred to the occasion as "The Last Supper."

❊ ❊ ❊

To give you an idea of how practical John Belk was I will tell you about an incident that could have been catastrophic, but John saved the day and our pride.

We took our wives on a trip to Egypt in 1989. The sightseeing and history was just wonderful and they even had a place where you could rent camels for a ride in the desert. Of course John and I had to have this manly experience so we rented two camels and took off into the desert. John looked rather ungainly with his long legs dangling off the camel. The sand dunes were very hilly there and you could get turned around in a hurry. However, the camels would only walk one mile per hour so we weren't worried. Besides, John was an Eagle Scout.

We had been gone almost an hour when we realized that we were completely lost and without a man-made thing in sight. Finally, John said he thought those were religious camels and opined that if we dropped the reins they would go back to Mecca. We did and they did! Fortunately Mecca and the camel stables were in the same direction! Thank goodness for John Belk's common sense.

Shared by Duke Kimbrell, one of John's golfing buddies:

My relationship with John Belk began in the mid-seventies. We would fly my airplane down every year to the Masters Tournament. We would usually be with Stuart Dickson, Jay Johnson, Johnny Harris, and Louis Rose. When you got these guys together the jokes would fly all evening long and John Belk would be the principal spokesperson!

The most humorous and enjoyable golfing trip I ever took was with John when we went to Scotland. There are no golf carts over there and the grass grows knee high in the rough. John was in his early eighties, but he walked the whole course and never complained or missed a beat. We played eighteen holes every day for six days! It wore me out, but John was never fatigued. He had high energy and much stamina.

Whenever John got a chance, he would introduce me by saying, "This is old Duke. When he's out of town he tells people he's from Charlotte. But when somebody knows him he has to admit that he's from Gastonia."

Shared by Jay Johnson, long-time friend and legal advisor to John:

I moved my family and my law practice to Charlotte in 1980 and John Belk was on the forefront of Charlotte's growth. Fortunately we became business associates and long-time best friends. Hopefully I can share some insight about this remarkable human being.

John was an outstanding basketball player and received an offer to play for Duke University. His father, William Henry, was a staunch Presbyterian and wasted no time in reminding John that he had accepted a scholarship to play for Davidson College, a college funded by the Presbyterian Church. It worked out okay since John became a star player there.

John was fifty years old when he and Claudia married and Claudia was about seventeen years his junior. Claudia's mother was also named Claudia and when John took them both to Quail Hollow Country

Club, one of John's friends congratulated the wrong Claudia.

John was a member of the World Business Council and he and Claudia went on trips all over the world. Some of the members of this organization had their 'trophy wives' with them. When one of his friends appeared with a new wife, John quipped, "I married my second wife first. Second wives always seem to be treated much better than the first wife."

❀ ❀ ❀

John and Claudia were delighted when their daughter, Mary Claudia came along. When she was about six years old, Claudia asked John to explain Thanksgiving to Mary Claudia. He said, "Mary Claudia, Thanksgiving is the day we have the Christmas Parade."

❀ ❀ ❀

Court-ordered busing to achieve racial balance in the schools was imposed by Judge James B. McMillan. While John was no fan of Judge McMillan, he worked hard to ensure that integration was accomplished peacefully. John's differences with Judge McMillan stemmed from the judge's long, drawn-out proceeding that delayed the construction of a freeway that was important for the city. These differences became fairly evident to everyone. On social occasions when the two might be seated at the same table, Claudia would sit between them.

On one such occasion, the judge looked across the table at John and said. "Why does everybody tell me that you refer to me as an SOB?"

John replied, "I never called you an SOB, but how can you read my mind so well?"

❀ ❀ ❀

John served his country in two wars, World War II and the Korean War. While serving in Korea, he received notice from the Army that he was considered AWOL. He simply wrote across the notice, 'Come and get me' and returned it to the Department of the Army.

❦ ❦ ❦

When John shipped out to Korea in 1950 he entrusted a German pistol, a World War II trophy, to Harry Howard, a Belk store partner in Augusta, Georgia. Years later, after John was mayor, Howard returned the pistol to John and he threw it into his suitcase without any further thought. Later he flew by private plane to Teterboro Airport just outside New York City to attend an American Management meeting. After the meeting he was attempting to fly out of LaGuardia by commercial plane. As he passed through security, the pistol was discovered and he was firmly escorted to a detention area by a New York City policeman. At first, John thought he had found a new friend as the two exchanged old war stories. All the while John was wondering how in the world he was going to get out of the mess without national publicity.

The policeman gave him two options; he could spend the night in jail and face a judge the following morning or relinquish the gun on the spot. He really liked the pistol and it was valued at over $2,000. But after talking to Jake Goodman, then the Charlotte Chief of Police, and to John Green, attorney for Belk Store Services, he decided to walk away from the gun. The smile on the policeman's face convinced John that the policeman had developed the same fondness for the gun that he had.

❦ ❦ ❦

John loved to confound reporters. His answer to a reporter's question was usually quick and diverting.

A reporter once asked, "Mayor Belk, what do you think about neighborhoods?"

He said, "I'm in favor of neighborhoods, I grew up in one."

When John was nearing the end of his fourth term as mayor of Charlotte, a television political reporter bugged John about when he would announce his run for reelection. John first told him to contact his secretary, "She charges $1,000 per hour for consultation." Undaunted, the reporter persisted in asking if and when John would be announcing his bid for reelection. John relented and told the reporter that he would hold an exclusive press conference just for him at Belk Store Services and gave him the date and time. The reporter showed up and everything was in place including a camera, lights, and a microphone.

John stepped up to the lectern and stated, "Ladies and gentlemen, it is my pleasure to introduce you to one of the finest candidates for mayor that has ever run for the office. He knows the city well and has a great speaking voice. He knows the problems of the city and studies and understands city council. The candidate I am referring to is this reporter."

The reporter yelled, "Cut, cut, cut," and abruptly left the room.

❖ ❖ ❖

I'll leave you with this last glimpse of John Belk, the encourager and politician. One Sunday I was standing with John outside the church before Sunday services began. As someone approached John he congratulated him or her.

The person smiled and said, "Thanks, Mr. Belk!"

He gave the same greeting to the next person who replied, "Thanks for remembering, John." After the third person came by with the same exchange, I asked what he was congratulating them for.

He said, "I don't know, but I read somewhere that eight out of ten people think they have done something special and the other two don't really count!"

Shared by John's long-time friend, Tom Haggai, professional speaker and IGA Global president:

John Belk was one of my top friends since 1961. He would trust you, was trustworthy, would never violate a confidence, and would give you the benefit of his opinions. We worked in Boy Scouting together and John was my first key supporter when I transitioned from the clergy into a full-time speaking career.

As my speaking career began to skyrocket, John told me he was concerned that I would get a "big head." I told John I was worried about him since he was president of an organization that had over 300 stores and was not yet mature enough to get married! John said, "You trumped me there, Tom!"

John was funny. His humor was a key to John's success in politics, business, and life in general. Sometimes he misspoke, but he usually knew what he was doing, like Yogi Berra. John was always confident and positive and had great faith in God.

When he couldn't complete the airport during his last term as mayor, he became chair of the Airport Authority. If something didn't work out as planned, John figured it was God's will and he'd try another approach!

Shared by John's long-time friend, Ed Weisiger:

John and I played a lot of golf together over the years and I am proud to have had that time with him. Agnes and I loved being around John and Claudia. When we played golf, I was fortunate to be able to find John's lost golf balls that he often sliced or hooked into the rough.

"Ed, you're the best seeing eye dog I ever saw," he often stated. It was close to the best compliment I ever got from him.

❖ ❖ ❖

Only on one occasion to my memory did John compliment one of my golf shots. We were on the tee box on a par three, 175-yard hole. I hit an excellent shot.

John exclaimed, "Ed, that's a great shot!"

I replied, "I think it was since it was a hole in one!"

❋ ❋ ❋

Several people know the story John would tell on himself about his golfing skill. There is disagreement whether the incident happened at the Charlotte Country Club or at Augusta National, but it is of little consequence.

John was evidently playing pretty poorly one day and he remarked to the new caddy, "I guess you think I'm the worst golfer in this club?"

"No, sir," the caddy replied, "that would be Mr. John Belk!"

Shared by Congresswoman Sue Myrick:

John Belk was a good friend to me and most everyone in Charlotte. He loved our city and worked tirelessly to make it a better place to work, play, and live. I admired him for many things, but especially the way he could tease and sometimes confuse news reporters.
One day when he was mayor, John was waiting to do an interview with a television reporter. Ed, my husband, and I were standing around with some other people when the reporter approached John with the first question.

John seemed not to hear him, and then asked, "Are you speaking to me?"

After the startled reported recovered from shock, he said, "Well, certainly, Mr. Mayor."

It was typical of John Belk to put people off balance in a humorous, but gentle way.

Shared by long-time friend, Gretchen Prendergast:

My husband, Chuck, and I value our association with John and Claudia and have many fond memories of our times together. I will share two of them with you. One demonstrates how John could command any situation and the other demonstrates his perpetual positive attitude.

John graciously invited Chuck and me to Augusta National and while there insisted that I play the course with them. Of course, this was a men-only club. Nevertheless, John took us both to the course and we were assigned a caddy and off we went. This must have rattled the caddy because he kept getting our clubs mixed up and placed in the wrong bags.

John finally had enough of this and addressed the caddy, "You ever caddy before?"

The caddy was horrified and replied, "Yes, sir, Mr. Belk."

He did a better job for the rest of the game.

❦ ❦ ❦

Early one Saturday morning, John called us and suggested that we take our daughter, Camie, and their daughter, Mary Claudia, to Andrew Jackson State Park for a picnic. We agreed to the idea and John was to pick us up at 11:30 a.m. At about 11:30 a.m. it began raining like a monsoon! When John pulled up to our house, I suggested we try on another day. John confidently said not to worry and that the weather would be fine. We all piled into the automobile and just as we pulled into the state park, the skies cleared and the sun came out! John said, "I told you it would be alright!"

John was fond of calling Claudia his "sweet ole girl." He was never old in his mind or spirit. Even into his middle eighties, rain or shine, he would be the first to the tee box.

Shared by Tommy Norman, CEO of Norcom Properties:

Most of what I remember about John were the social events and dinners Patty and I would share with him and Claudia. They were always incredibly enjoyable and lighthearted occasions and we never ran out of conversation. Without exception, John would greet me with two questions; "Tom, how you doing? And, how's your mother?" His concern for you and your family was genuine and a real asset for his success.

❖ ❖ ❖

John was a funny guy. At one event where John spoke, I overheard a member of the audience remark, "You know, John is an absolute comedian and doesn't even know it."

I think he not only knew it, but planned it that way.

John's memory, the twinkle in his eyes, and his zest for life made all of us feel as if we were his finest friend!

Shared by John Medlin, retired chairman and chief executive of Legacy Wachovia Corporation:

John was a board member of our company for over thirty years, from 1958 to 1990. Especially in his later years, John was prone to doze off in board meetings. But the moment something of importance came up, he would perk up and ask a pertinent question.

His business knowledge was vast and you could never tell John anything he didn't already know. There was one notable exception I recall:

Our headquarters were in Winston Salem and that's where most of our board meetings were held. For years John would speak up during a meeting and say, "I want to make a motion that we move the headquarters to Charlotte."

I would say, "I'm sorry, but that is out of order, Mr. Belk."

Many years later in April of 2001, and after both of us had retired from the board, the current board chair informed me that they had voted to merge with First Union whose headquarters were in Charlotte. I called John at home at 7:30 a.m. before he could learn the news elsewhere and told him that his motion had finally been approved!

Shared by Jim McNair, a long-time friend:

One time John and Claudia and Marion and I drove to the ACC finals in Greensboro. It started snowing before the game and John suggested that we go home and watch the last half on television. I reminded him that he had the best four seats in the arena.

"Let's sell them to some of these young college boys who want to see the game." John gave them to me and said not to sell them for a penny over face value.

When the boys sat down next to Joe Robinson, Belk's chief financial officer, who had seats next to John's, Joe told them to get out of Mr. Belk's seats. They were intimidated, but showed him John's ticket stubs and they were allowed to stay.

* * *

John was an unflappable person. One time John, Mark Erwin, and I flew in a private plane to Augusta National to see the Masters Tournament. The weather was threatening to rain, but we took a chance and left early in the morning. Sure enough we hit terrible weather at Augusta and couldn't land. After forty-five minutes of circling, John said we could have been in Miami by then.

We flew back to Charlotte, got into Mark's van and drove back to Augusta. When we arrived several hours later, the tournament had been temporarily suspended, but someone suggested that we walk to the Belk-sponsored picnic. It was at the far end of the course. We sloshed over there only to find that it was closed. We trudged back to the crowded clubhouse and ate a sandwich. As we finished, it was announced that the tournament was cancelled for the day due to bad weather. We had spent twelve hours and made two trips to Augusta and never saw a ball! John took it all in good humor.

Shared by Jerry Orr, Charlotte aviation director:

John was always a favorite of mine. We worked together when he was mayor and afterwards as he chaired the Airport Advisory Committee. John made me feel like a son and was always sending notes and encouraging me and prodding me to keep moving forward. He used stories and humor to make his points and persuade others to agree with him. He was a master of overstating the obvious and knew how to deflect criticism.

❊ ❊ ❊

In 1975 Josh Birmingham, the airport manager at that time, asked me to write a speech for John. I'm an engineer, not a speech writer. I researched the topic and worked for three days writing that speech. I typed it up and gave it to John. He looked at it, folded it up and put it in his pocket, and never used a word of it.

❊ ❊ ❊

When John was mayor, he would often pull up to the airport and park at the curb, ignoring his reserved parking space fifty feet away. He would drop his keys off with me and my job was to move his car to the space reserved for the mayor. This continued until Eddie Knox became mayor, then John would dutifully park in the mayor's space. We had to set up two mayor spaces.

Shared by Ray Killian, Jr. who was mentored by John:

I've known John Belk since childhood. He was a friend, mentor, and Sunday school leader. He was always so considerate of others, remembering their birthdays, anniversaries, and new births in the family. He was also an incredible historian and could talk for hours about history and politics.

❊ ❊ ❊

I have always loved to play golf and the main goal I developed as I became a young adult was to play at Augusta National Golf Club. The only person I knew who had a membership at Augusta was John Belk. Fear finally gave way to desire and I broached the subject with John.

"Mr. Belk. I just want you to know that sometime in my life I want to play golf at Augusta National."

"Well, Ray," John replied, "that's what everyone wants to do!"

I stuttered a reply that if there was ever an opportunity, I would be delighted to play there with him and left thinking I had blown my only chance. About two months later, John grabbed me at Sunday school and invited me to play golf at Augusta National. John, Joe, and Ed Haggar of the Haggar Slacks organization, and I played a round on a spring day. We had a wonderful time, but I noticed that John's driver and putter were well over twenty years old.

When I got home, I bought John the best new driver and putter money could buy and took them over to his home. He opened the box, hesitated, and then said, "Are you trying to tell me how poorly I play golf?"

"No, no. I just think it is time to upgrade your technology," I replied.

I never knew if he was offended or just teasing, but knowing John, I suspect the latter!

John invited me to play at Augusta National again. This time we played with two of John's friends, investment bankers from New York. I must say, I thought his new driver and putter improved his game!

Shared by Frank Matthews, a Belk store partner:

I represent the second generation of my family to work in the Belk business. My father and uncles worked with John's family in the late 1800s. Mr. William Henry Belk taught me a lot about the retail business, life, how to be a gentleman, and how to be a good Christian.

Mr. Belk sent my father to manage the Gastonia store and soon invited him to become a store partner and enjoy the fruits of ownership. Later, my father trained two of his brothers who then became partners in Belk stores in Georgia. My father and uncles worked very hard to make their stores successful. This owner/partner relationship was the genius of William Henry Belk. Ownership allowed him to expand and ensured high productivity and sales.

John and I were contemporaries and both of us came into the business about the same time. John spent two tours in the military, one in World War II and one in the Korean War. He could spin yarns all day long about his tours of duty. He was also an industry leader in the department store business. One of his best attributes was his ability to look into the future and anticipate what would be happening in the department store business. He was always a jump ahead of his competitors and was good at working with his partners to get agreements.

In the mid to late nineties, John and his brother, Tom, realized that the existing business model would no longer work well. They proposed a consolidation of the partner stores so they could compete with the emerging conglomerates, having more purchasing power as a group than as individual stores.

* * *

John could solve problems. Sometimes he would say, "That problem is like dancing with a gorilla. You can dance, but you just can't quit dancing."

He was patient with everyone, except reporters sometimes. Reporters could get tough on John, but he always came out on top. Once when rumors were circulating that Belk was closing its downtown Columbia, South Carolina, store a Columbia-based reporter called John and said, "I understand that's a done deal."

John handled it this way, "Yes, we have a store in Dunn, North Carolina, and that store does extremely well. Goodbye."

Shared by Tod Thorne, an admirer of John Belk:

My wife, Patty, and I were at a fund raiser for Al Gore at Cammie Harris's home several years ago and we were seated next to John and Claudia near the swimming pool.

A reporter came up and asked John if it were true that he gave 28 million dollars to Davidson College. John said that it was true.

"And is it true that you played basketball for Davidson?"

"Yes," John replied.

"I'll bet you were a good player."

"Yes, I guess I was pretty good," John answered. As the reporter walked away, John leaned over to us and said, "When you're as old as I am, you can claim anything you want because there's no one left to dispute you."

Shared by Leroy Mayne, Boy Scout executive for Mecklenburg County for 18 years:

John Montgomery Belk was one of the most honored adult Boy Scout leaders in our nation. He was an Eagle Scout, led an Explorer Post for years, established Boy Scout troops while serving in Korea, and served on the Mecklenburg County Executive Board and the National Board for the Boy Scouts of America. He was honored with the Silver Beaver Award for local leadership, the Silver Antelope Award for regional leadership, and the Silver Buffalo Award for national leadership. As national treasurer on the National Council, John helped guide the organization through two major challenges that eventually were ruled in our favor by the U.S. Supreme Court. I know of no other person who has contributed so much to scouting in America and it was an honor to have worked with him.

❋ ❋ ❋

My first meeting with John was scheduled in September 1989, in his office on a Friday morning. Hurricane Hugo arrived the night before and the Charlotte area was devastated. Trees were down all over town, the roads seemed impassable, electricity was out and so was telephone service. By Friday morning, National Guardsmen were about the only people in the streets and I couldn't reach John by telephone. I couldn't get past a block or two, let alone make it to his office.

Several days went by as the community slowly recovered. By coincidence I ran into John in an elevator downtown so I introduced myself. John looked at me rather sternly and said, "Where where you? We had an appointment and you missed it!" I never knew if he was serious or joking, but I never missed another meeting with John Belk.

❊ ❊ ❊

In the early nineties, John was going to attend the World Scout Jamboree in Australia. John's secretary called me to find out where they could get a uniform to fit John. She must not have known that Belk stores had the exclusive rights for selling Boy Scout uniforms and related items. I called the national distributor to get the uniform he needed and took it to John. The national distributor then asked John if the Scout Council could pilot test uniform sales at our office site. John agreed to allow it for six months. It has now been sixteen years and our sales have become a key revenue source for the council.

❊ ❊ ❊

John stayed active in scouting all of his life. In his eighties John still went to major scout functions. I remember he went with John Ashworth into the circle, dancing to Indian tom toms at the National Jamboree at Fort A.P. Hill military base in Virginia.

❊ ❊ ❊

You had no clue when John Belk, in his later years, would show up at a meeting. Even the national council never knew when he would show up at their national conventions. He attended a local executive board meeting once when his nephew, Tim, was the chairman. He sat in the back of the room, ostensibly to support Tim, and immediately picked up a newspaper and read it pretty much throughout the meeting.

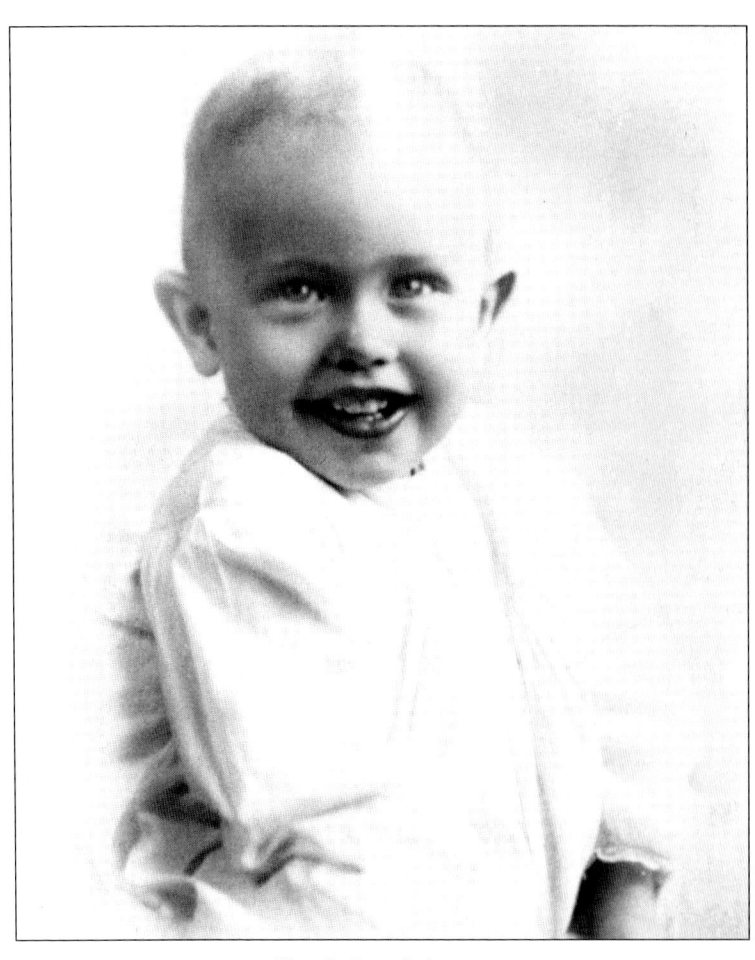

*All smiles from the beginning
John Montgomery Belk*

Young John Belk

Davidson College days, Class of 1943. Front seat–Bob Dalton and John Belk. Rumble seat–Roslyn Reid Harris and Peggy Parsley

John Belk (center kneeling). Captain of the Davidson College Basketball team. 1939–1943

*Willaim Henry and Mary Irwin Belk Family
Standing left to right–Tom, Henderson, Henry, and John
Seated left to right–William Henry, Mary Irwin, Sarah, and Irwin*

Emerging businessman, John Belk

*Second Lieutenant John Belk,
1943–1945
U.S. Army Infantry, World War II*

*First Lieutenant John Belk,
1950–1952
Korean War*

*Claudia and John Belk's wedding day.
February 20, 1971, Durham, NC*

Mr. Mayor
1969–1977

We won!
Claudia and John, 1975

John, Claudia and newborn Mary Claudia, 1973

Mayor Belk and City Councilman Fred D. Alexander, 1975

John in the rough

Johnny Cash and Mayor Belk, 1973

President Gerald Ford and John Belk, 1981

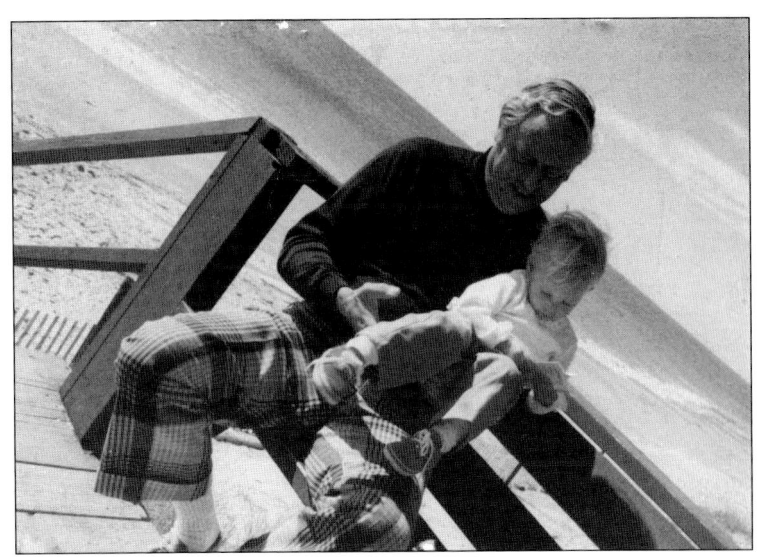

John and Mary Claudia

*The John Belk Freeway is dedicated
John, Mary Claudia, Claudia, Governor Jim Hunt,
Bill Roberson, and former Mayor Eddie Knox*

A light moment with Billy
John Belk and Billy Graham, 1978

Golfing at Augusta National
Jim McNair, John Belk, Mark Erwin, and Robert Pittenger

A Presidential moment
President Ronald Reagan with Claudia and John

A noble moment
John with Prime Minister Margaret Thatcher

All business
John at Belk Stores Services

Belk Stores Leaders
William Henry Belk (bust), Tom Belk, and John Belk, 1987

Family portrait
Claudia, John, Mary Claudia

A formal evening in 1986
Claudia and John

The North Pole
John and Claudia, 1996

John's three favorite sports

A Boy Scout Leader forever

1998 Rotary's Excellence in Leadership awarded to John Belk
Nominated by Tony Zeiss
Leroy Robinson, Tony Zeiss, John Belk

A formal event
Rail and Sarah Brinson, Claudia and John Belk, and Tom Hayes

John the Grandfather, 2005
Mary Claudia, James Pilon (born February 22, 2004), and John

A devoted couple
Claudia and John

Shared by Tony Zeiss, president of Central Piedmont Community College:

John told me about his first night at home with Claudia. "After we were married, I moved in with Claudia because she had the better place. Her bed was one of those that was expecting a rain, you know, with a canopy. It was far too short for me and my feet hung over it."

"I can't sleep in this!" I told her.

"I never expected you when I bought it," she replied.

"I never asked her who she expected!"

❖ ❖ ❖

I once told John that we were both fortunate to marry beautiful women. John said, "Yes, and I really liked Claudia's intellect."

❖ ❖ ❖

John and I usually paired up on the annual Charlotte Chamber intercity visits. We both loved history and we talked about it a great deal during free time. On our visit to Dallas several years ago, I asked John if he'd like to walk down and see the Texas Book Depository building where Lee Harvey Oswald shot John F. Kennedy from a window. It had been turned into a museum.

"You bet," John replied.

We walked about eight or ten city blocks and I had a hard time keeping up with those long legs of his. While in the museum, John was all business. Afterward, we discussed what we saw, the credibility or lack thereof of the Warren Commission's Report and other noteworthy historical things including John's acquaintance with Kennedy.

On the way back he told me this heart-rending story:

"Sherman's troops drowned my grandfather, Abel Belk, down there at Gill's Creek located a short distance from his father Tom Belk's home. Abel lived in the Waxhaw community bordering the North Carolina and South Carolina border. Those Yankees were combing the countryside for anything they could steal, plunder, or burn. The South had mostly given up and there was no protection for anyone. Grandfather and a neighbor fled their homes hoping the raiders would follow them and not destroy their homes or steal their property. They hid near Gill's creek.

The Yankees found my grandfather and his neighbor and speculated that since they were able-bodied men and were not in the Confederate Army, they must be involved with the barrels of gold that were rumored to be hidden in the area. Of course, they were just farmers and there was no gold.

Sherman's troops were probably unsupervised so they dragged my grandfather and his neighbor into the river and pushed them under at gun point to try to get them to tell where the mines were. Each time the Yankees would let them up for air, my grandfather and his neighbor would emphasize that they were farmers and knew nothing about any gold. Finally, those Feds drowned them both.

The neighbor's wife sent a letter to my grandmother telling her what had happened and that she had a wagon, but the Yankees had taken her horses. She suggested that if my grandmother had any horses, her farm hand would bring them back and they would retrieve the bodies for proper burial. Grandmother and the horses went over to the river to retrieve the men. This incident left my grandmother a widow with three young sons to manage their small farm. Two and a half year old William Henry, my father was one of the three children."

I told John that war is hell and that I was sorry to hear about that loss in his family. John then told me that Belk stores didn't celebrate Decoration Day, now known as Memorial Day, because it was a Yankee holiday!

As with most things of an historical nature, he was right.

❋ ❋ ❋

John told me this story the last time I saw him. "There was this man, John Smith, who was on death row in the dead of winter back in the forties. The warden told him he could order anything he wanted for his last meal which was coming up the next evening.

"Do you mean it, warden?" he asked. The warden assured him that was their policy. "Great. I'll have watermelon then."

"Why we can't get any watermelons until next summer," exclaimed the warden.

"I'll wait," John Smith said.

❋ ❋ ❋

John once told me about a farmer who had cleared his land and eventually built it into a very beautiful and productive farm. The farmer's friend remarked that the farmer should be grateful for what the Lord had given him. The farmer replied that he was grateful, but that his friend should have seen this place when the Lord owned it by himself!

❋ ❋ ❋

It seemed as though I was always asking John Belk for money to support worthy causes, mostly at Central Piedmont Community College, of course. After several generous gifts to establish scholarships and to support the Claudia Watkins Belk Center for Criminal Justice, I noticed that John always gave me one half of what I asked him to give. In 2004, we needed to increase our scholarship endowment and establish an equipment endowment and John was my first prospect. I explained our value to the community and our needs and asked John for ten million dollars, hoping for five. I also told him that for a gift of that size we would be pleased to name the entire downtown campus in his honor. "Why would I want my name on anything else? It's already on hundreds of stores," John countered. He had slipped out of the noose that time.

A year later I approached John to help the college develop its part of the Little Sugar Creek Greenway. I was optimistic since John had tried to develop Little Sugar Creek when he was mayor and he had helped us resurrect the idea and kick it off four years earlier. I knew we needed a minimum of $500,000 for the project, so I planned to ask John for a million.

When we met on the project, he and Leroy Robinson were very cordial as usual and I could tell they liked the architect's rendering of the John Montgomery Belk Plaza. I asked him for the million dollars. You never knew how John was going to react to a request for money, but this reaction was a new one.

John leaned forward and said, "It's nice, but where will I find the money?"

"If you let me look at your books, I'll show you," I replied.

John gave me that little grin and his eyes twinkled. He gave me $500,000 for the project!

Chapter Two
John Belk's Wit

There is no question that John Belk was one of the wittiest men in Charlotte or anywhere else for that matter. He was beloved for his quick sense of humor and general good nature and he is fondly remembered for the same. It seems that in so many of my conversations someone invariably refers to John Belk and one or more of his antics or funny stories. Here are some examples of the witty things people remember about John.

Shared by Johnny Belk, John's nephew and president and chief operating officer, Belk, Inc.:

When I moved to Belk Stores Services, I had not had much experience with Uncle John, especially in a business setting. I remember being amazed at his quick wit and his vast repertoire of jokes which could fit all circumstances.

David Burkhalter was working at Belk Stores Services after serving as city manager under Uncle John. No one really knew what David did, but I assumed he gathered jokes and witticisms to feed to John. I later recognized that Uncle John gathered, or more likely created, his own material.

Shared by Cammie Harris, Charlotte entrepreneur and long-time friend of John:

One of the endearing things about John was that he could take teasing as well as he dished it out. I well remember a couple of incidents that were wonderfully amusing at the time and still tickle me today.

Several years back, Quail Hollow Country Club was hosting its annual "Men's Only Day." Every male member was expected to attend the festivities and some serious money was raised for community causes. We had a rule that if you were absent, you were fined $50. John had missed six years in a row, but showed up on this occasion. I was one of the organizers for the event and the moment I saw John walk in, I hailed him to the microphone and began to harass him for his past absences. "John, it's time to pay up," I told him. The crowd affirmed my statement in a raucous manner.

He pulled out his wallet and handed it to me. There was nothing but a few ones and fives in it. "I'm afraid that won't be enough, John," I badgered.

John replied by saying, "Oh, that's the wrong wallet!"

He then pulled out another wallet with $600 in it. The crowd went wild over his anticipation of the fine and his ability to ride along with the fun.

* * *

We always had a skit at the "Men's Only Day" and I can still see John wearing a pink tutu in the Snow White and Seven Dwarfs production. He was a good sport!

During another "Men's Only Day" skit John played Robin and Stuart Dickson played Batman. Of course they were both dressed for the occasion which brought belly laughs from the crowd. But the climax of the event was when they had to jump into the bat mobile, which was a decorated go-cart. John had to fold up to get in behind Stuart. Stuart's feet wouldn't reach the pedals so John had to operate the gas and brakes, while Stuart steered the machine. They drove all over the club, much to the delight of everyone involved!

Shared by Mark Erwin, former ambassador and long-time friend of John:

John once told me about the time he was presiding over a city council public hearing regarding the need to expand Providence Road and whether they should invoke the eminent domain authority. One man began to rant and rave about the issue and was getting out of hand with his insults and threats.

Finally, the mayor interrupted, "Excuse me, Henry, (not his real name), but have you stopped beating your wife?"

The man was astonished and stammered, "Why, John, I've never beaten my wife. Why would you say such a thing?"

John softened his voice, "Oh, I know that, Henry. I just needed to slow you down."

John was a master at defusing situations with humor and the unexpected. He would tell jokes and stories, but didn't really care whether you understood them. He cared whether they were effective in changing the subject, eliminating a problem, or distracting someone for the fun of it.

Shared by Chris William, host of the *Carolina Business Review* television program:

I have been privileged to host *Carolina Business Review* for many years and one of my most unforgettable moments occurred when John Belk was a guest along with Bill Disher of the Lance Corporation and Johnny Harris of Lincoln Harris. We had been talking about business in general and about labor more specifically. I finally asked Mr. Belk how he would handle the unionization of Belk stores if it ever came to that. He paused, and then said, "I don't know much about unions, but my daddy grew up in Union County!" He never answered the question and I proceeded to go in another direction with the conversation.

Shared by Jim McNair, long-time friend of John:

I was with John at the Charlotte Convention Center when he was mayor. A preacher walked up to John and introduced himself. "I am John D. Oxindine from Atlanta, Georgia."

John said, "I know where Atlanta is, but where's Georgia?"

The preacher grinned and retorted, "Ah, they told me you always fool around!"

❊ ❊ ❊

On another occasion, John left my house and slipped on the icy steps. His long arms and legs flailed like a windmill and he landed on his head. A knot the size of a chicken egg swelled up on his head.

Holding his head, he looked up at my wife, Marion, and said, "I hope you've got a good lawyer."

"I do," she countered. "It's Claudia!"

"You've got me there!" John responded.

❊ ❊ ❊

John told me once that he never had much love for politicians and lawyers and he'd be darned if he hadn't married both of them (Claudia of course)!

❊ ❊ ❊

Once I bummed a ride with John who was flying on a large private jet owned by the National Distillery, taking the board to the Super Bowl in California. After a while, a gentleman asked me if I would like to play cards with him. Of course, I agreed and found him to be a congenial person. As I took a restroom break I asked John who my card playing friend was.

"Oh, he works for the telephone company," John replied. After we landed some four hours later, my telephone company friend handed me his card. He was Chairman of the Board for AT&T!

❊ ❊ ❊

John wasn't very patient with poor service in restaurants. We took our families to Aspen once for Christmas. We went to a popular restaurant and waited for 45 minutes to get service.

Finally, John spoke up. "We're out of here," and he stood up to leave and we followed.

At that time the waitress ran over and said, "Oh, I'm sorry, I was just coming over."

John said, "You're a great waitress; you out waited me!"

Shared by Louis Rose, one of John's long-time friends:

John was one of my best friends and a wonderful person. We celebrated our anniversaries together for decades. After John's last term as mayor, a reporter asked, "Are you going to run for mayor again, Mr. Belk?" John said he wasn't.

"Why not? Do you have a health issue?" the reporter asked.

"No, but the voters might be sick of me!" he replied.

Shared by Susan Jamison, John's financial advisor:

John was almost never at a loss for words. He owned a large piece of land south of town and a small Methodist church wanted him to donate one acre so they could expand their building. He wouldn't give them the acre. I worked out a land swap, but he wouldn't do that either, citing that his acre was worth more than their acre. So I asked him what he would do when he got to heaven and Saint Peter asked him why he didn't give that church an acre of land. "I will tell him they weren't Presbyterian and they didn't want to pay for it!"

Shared by Harvey Gantt, long-time colleague in local government:

I worked with John for three years while I was on city council and he was mayor. We worked on numerous projects for Charlotte over twenty years or more.

When I won my first race for city council and was being sworn in, my wife, Cindy, and our very young son, Adam, joined me at the council chambers in the old court house for the ceremony. After being formally inducted into the council, each councilman was allowed to make some remarks. Adam was perfectly quiet during my remarks, but when a couple of Republican councilmen followed with their remarks, our baby Adam squalled loudly.

John said, "Well, Harvey, I see your son is a Democrat!"

❄ ❄ ❄

I used to tease John about his basketball skills at Davidson College by telling him how impressed I was that he had been such a fine athlete back in the forties. I would then mention to John that I played a little football in my time. This went on for years until John came back from playing golf at Augusta National one time and said, "I ran into an old friend of yours named Cephas Young who now works at Augusta. He says he knew you when you played football and told me you weren't nearly as good as you thought you were!" I stopped teasing John, who was, by the way, a fine basketball player.

Shared by Sydnor Thompson, long-time friend of John:

Several years ago my cousin from Virginia owned a department store and wanted to sell it. He asked me to connect him with John to see if he would have any interest in buying the store. I set up the meeting. We had barely finished the pleasantries when John abruptly asked how much money my cousin wanted for his store. The question surprised him, but he rallied and said he wanted five million dollars for the store. John said he would send someone up to look it over.

After John's person visited the store and reviewed its books, John told my cousin he would pass on the purchase of the store. A month later the store went bankrupt! Every time John saw me since that time he would announce, "Sydnor is the man that tried to sell me a bankrupt store!"

Shared by Robert Pittenger, CEO of the Pittenger Company and NC State Senator:

In the 1990's when I was hosting the Charlotte Foreign Policy Forums, we brought in Margaret Thatcher, former Prime Minister of the United Kingdom. I asked John to be the emcee. He gave a twenty-minute introduction and people began to snicker, then laughed, and finally wailed as he told his anecdotes and basically murdered the King's English. John perceived the situation correctly and explained to Lady Thatcher, "Over here we have the King's English, American English, and John Belk's English!"

As I walked out to the airplane the next day, Lady Thatcher commented, "Robert, you tell John Belk that I shall never forget his introduction, at least the part I understood!"

My respect and gratitude for John Belk is unequaled. My real estate investment company wouldn't be where it is without John Belk who was an early investor and supporter.

Shared by David Zimmerman, long-time admirer of John:

I heard these two stories about 25 years ago when I sat at a table with John and Leroy Robinson. The subject of the relationship between John and Pat Hall came up and the stories came out. Apparently John and Pat, who was a "wheel" in Charlotte for years, loved to play practical jokes on one another.

When John and Claudia moved into a beautiful home on Hempstead Place in Charlotte, unknown to John and Claudia, Pat sent out a formal invitation to many of their friends inviting them to a surprise housewarming party. On the designated day and time, the guests began showing up and John and Claudia had no idea what was going on. Shortly afterward, Pat showed up with a truck filled with food, drinks, and a band for the occasion.

Pat built Carowinds and his office there had a small courtyard. The story is that every time he would dismiss an executive, Pat would place a small tombstone in the courtyard with the person's name on it. One day, Pat invited John out to his office to show him his latest addition to the graveyard. There stood a new tombstone that read: "John Ivey Belk!" John was a competitor of Ivey's department store.

Judy Rozelle used to work at Carowinds with Pat and she told me about the time that Pat and John were attending a Billy Graham revival. Apparently John had a large check from a business deal the two had completed. According to Judy, John threw the check in the offering plate as it passed by. Pat recognized what happened and ran after the ushers to get it back!

Shared by Joan Zimmerman, long-time friend of John:

I served on the airport authority when John was the chairman. At one meeting, while discussing signage for the airport, John said, "You've got to be careful with signage and make sure it is not misinterpreted. We almost had a riot at our CHA-L-ston (Charleston) store once. One sign in the window said, Women's Dresses, Half Off. Another sign said, Men's Pants, Way Down."

Everyone at the table laughed, except me, and I desperately wanted to. He then said, "You didn't like that very much did you, Joan?"

I replied, "Not a whole lot."

* * *

At another meeting, we were receiving a presentation from some Philadelphia architects and they went on and on until John spoke up.

"Does anybody know how to spot a man with kidney problems?"

Dutifully, someone responded, "No, John."

"Well, he goes around all the time with yellar shoes!"

Then promptly, he thanked the architects, told them we got the picture, and the presentation was over.

※ ※ ※

Community leader Pat Hall and John were very good friends and Pat used to stop by the Belk headquarters downtown at least once a week for coffee. He wore the same hat every day and it came from Belk's. He'd walk into John's office, hang his hat on the tree stand, and they would chat away. John arranged for one of his assistants to swap Pat's hat with an identical hat only one-eighth size smaller each week. Of course Pat's hat began to sit higher and higher on his head until he figured it out!

Shared by Alex Coffin (from his book, *Brookshire and Belk, Businessmen in City Hall*, p. 132):

Just before the 1971 election campaign got serious, Bill Poe, who was chairman of the school board at the time, got a call from Mayor Belk. "May I come over to your office?" the mayor asked Poe, who readily agreed, yet wondered at the urgency of Belk's request.

A few minutes later, Belk got to Poe's office, which was in the Cameron Brown building. The mayor looked worried and clutched a large brown envelope tightly. "What's this all about?" Belk said, still with a worried look on his face.

Poe looked at an 8 by 10 photograph Belk pulled from the envelope. The picture showed a huge political billboard reading, "Bill Poe for mayor." It should be noted here that some people had suggested Poe should run for mayor, but he had expressed no interest.

It was then that Poe realized that Belk was pulling another one of his practical jokes. The sign was from Tampa, Florida, where the incumbent mayor, running for reelection, was named Bill Poe.

John's quick witticisms heard by many, provided by:

Jerry Orr:

One time I learned that John had a place at the beach. When I saw him next, I asked him how he liked his place at the beach. "They're all Yankees down where we have our place. I'm the only American in the bunch!"

Rolfe Neill:

Someone once asked John if he had lived in Charlotte all of his life. "I hope not!" John replied.

John once asked me if I knew why there were only three balls in a tennis can. "No." I answered.

"Because that is all they can hold," he replied.

Ralph Pitts:

John liked to say that politics is like shaving lotion: you can pat it and smell it, but don't drink it. It will ruin your perspective.

Bishop George Battle:

John once asked, "What do you tell a man with two black eyes? Nothing, he's already been told!"

Luther Moore:

"Everyone wants to go to heaven, but nobody wants to die. But everybody does."

Bill Disher:

Years ago while visiting one of his stores, John met a charming young woman who appeared to be in her early thirties. John asked her how long she had been with Belk.

"Thirty-five years!" she told him.

"Thirty-five years? That's amazing!" John exclaimed. "You're so young, how have you worked here for thirty-five years?"

"Overtime," she replied.

Alex Coffin (in his book, *Brookshire and Belk Businessmen in City Hall*, p. 151)**:**

Public officials live in a glass house and must appear at the front door. And you have to be dressed right.

Ann Fettner (in her 1977 September-October article in *Charlotte Magazine* page 28)**:**

His only remark about the Belk business empire concerns the days Elvis Presley drove a Belk truck in Mississippi. Later, when he met the then famous singer, he said to him, "I sure wish I'd taken 10% of you back then."

Presley replied, "Man, you could have had 90% of me then!"

Tony Zeiss:

John once told me, "I'm getting a little slow . . . it takes me an hour and a half to watch *60 Minutes!*"

I told John I would pray for him since he was going in for a hip replacement. "Don't pray for me," he advised. "Pray for the doctors!"

Whenever anyone would ask John how many people worked at Belk, he would say, "About half of them!"

"They took Leroy Robinson down to the hunting club and he didn't shoot a single guide."

"When I go bird hunting, I carry pocket scissors to cut the string they're tied to."

Once, we listened to Alan Greenspan at a civic function and John remarked, "I never understood a thing he said!"

John told me about the airport security person who asked him to take off his shoes. John replied, "You can have them, but they won't fit you."

A *Charlotte Observer* reporter once asked John, "What is your secret to your longevity?" John replied, "I got the right parents."

Chapter Three
John Belk's Wisdom

When writing about John Belk's wit and wisdom, it is often difficult to separate the two. John, like so many clever leaders, used humor to convey instruction or share his wisdom. This chapter is designed to illustrate a sampling of the wisdom that he so generously shared with the rest of us.

John Belk's Thoughts on "The Meaning of Life"
December 18, 2002

Webster's defines life as "the sequence of physical, mental, and spiritual experiences that make up the existence of an individual."

I believe the environment and people are the biggest factors affecting life, and your mother and father have the most influence in your life. They are the ones who instill the values and beliefs that make the most difference in the kind of person you will become and what kind of life you will lead.

I was closer to my mother than my daddy growing up, I guess because I was with her longer. Daddy ran the business, but my mother ran the house and together they gave us a good upbringing.

I'm thankful for my daddy for two important reasons—first, I wouldn't be here and second, I wouldn't have a job if it weren't for him. He found religion—he was a devout Christian and Presbyterian—and lived it the best he could. The things that meant the most to him were church, family, business, and his fellow man. He believed in God, patriotism, motherhood, and the people associated with him in his business and community involvements.

Outside of church, family, and business, the things that have been most meaningful to me in my life are basketball and the Boy Scouts. As a member of the Davidson College basketball team, I learned how to get along with people and depend upon others. I learned life lessons about partnership, leadership, teamwork, and the importance of participating in the game.

As a Boy Scout, I professed my belief in God, country, community, and family. I learned to obey the twelve Boy Scout laws—to be trustworthy, loyal, helpful, friendly, courteous, kind, obedient, cheerful, thrifty, brave, clean, and reverent. I learned to love and appreciate nature, respect the environment, and get along better with my fellow man.

I have found that there are many things that happen in life that we don't understand, and never will. So often, we are faced with situations when we can't tell for sure what is right or wrong. That's where our trust and faith in God and our religious beliefs are important. God is infinite in his wisdom, and we must turn to him to help us find the answers and the truth. I believe he has a purpose for each one of us and we have a choice of whether or not we want to fulfill his will.

At weddings and other special occasions, we often propose toasts to good health, good friends, and family. I think these are the most important things, outside of the Lord, that you could possibly have.

Shared by Johnny Belk, John's nephew, and president and chief operating officer, Belk, Inc.:

I didn't really know what to expect from Uncle John when I first began working with him, but I learned pretty quickly.

John sometimes used humor to divert, disarm, or confuse you. Generally, he was just trying to determine if you had done your homework and if you knew what you were talking about. He was a master at this.

He was also a master at letting people know how he felt about things. For example, we began to build a large presence on the Internet in the mid-nineties, years before retail sales over the Internet had taken off. After one of those initial briefings on our Internet sales performance, John said, "If you're losing money what good is it?"

He did not like to waste time. He would stand up and walk out of a meeting when he thought it should be over . . . whether it was or not. Of course, the meeting would generally end at that point.

When traveling with John, you wouldn't be late but once because he would leave without you. Unfortunately, I have had firsthand experience with this characteristic.

John could also be as accommodating and generous as the best of them. Once, when John was the Carrousel Parade's Grand Marshall, he invited my family and me to ride with him. We all rode in a pink Cadillac convertible. He had a nice way of sharing things with others.

Shared by Humpy Wheeler, immediate past president and general manager of NASCAR's Lowe's Motor Speedway:

I worked for a year as director of information under John Belk when he was mayor. One time a disgruntled man lambasted him during a city council meeting. John listened then said, "I'm sorry you feel that way, but I understand. By the way that is a nice tie you have on."

Later that evening, I asked, "Mayor, how could you be so nice to such a person?"

He said, "My daddy told me not to get upset when someone says something bad to you, but compliment them and say something nice."

This was simple wisdom and it worked.

Shared by Hugh McColl, retired CEO of Bank of America:

When I served as chairman of the Charlotte Uptown Development movement, John was serving as mayor. We had been working for months on a new zoning configuration that we believed would benefit the uptown area greatly. Of course the mayor was supportive of anything that would improve Charlotte.

I made the presentation of our vision, complete with maps and renderings. The city planner at the time was relatively new and kept interrupting the presentation and voicing his concerns or giving reasons that this or that wouldn't work. After a while, John said, "You better look out for that dog in the street." The planning director would look rather puzzled, but continued his negative comments. John said again, "You'd better look out for that dog in the street."

After three or four sequences of this same advice, the planning director finally acknowledged the mayor and asked, "What do you mean, I should look out for that dog in the street? What dog?"

"The one that's on that Mack truck that's about to run over you if you don't quit objecting to this proposal!" John replied.

The planning director sat down and kept quiet. The proposal passed with flying colors!

Shared by Ralph Pitts, executive vice president and general counsel, Belk Stores Services:

John was very good at anticipating questions, determining changes in the retail marketplace, and managing questions. He was known to some as the "Artful Dodger." If he received questions he didn't want to answer, he would artfully dodge those who asked the questions by giving responses they could not understand.

John and his brother, Tom, along with George Ivy developed the SouthPark mall when other people couldn't see its potential. Later, Belk bought out Ivey's share and owned the entire mall.

Editor's Note: John would also verbalize to others that which impressed him about people. He generally introduced Ralph Pitts by stating, "He earned 75 merit badges, was first in his class at Chapel Hill, and has triplets!"

Shared by Ray Killian, retired executive vice president, Belk Stores Services:

I served as personnel director of a Belk store in Charlotte for eleven years and another thirty-five years with Belk Stores Services and had an office next to John's office. When they first brought me to the corporate offices, I asked John what he wanted me to do. "That's what we brought you down here for," John replied.

In my first week at the corporate office, John needed something, but I didn't complete it in the time that he wanted it. John asked me for the project and I explained that I had been very busy and hadn't yet finished it. "Everyone is very busy," John replied. I was never late with another assignment John gave me.

As a businessman, John was good at anticipating things before others even thought about it. He knew the airport was a key to Charlotte's future long before anyone else recognized it. He also knew the Belk business model needed to consolidate before anyone else and he did it through family members and Belk partners and without any real leverage except his relationships and ability to see the bigger picture.

John loved Charlotte and never accepted a dollar for his services as mayor. He called people on their birthdays and recognized that each person was as important as were his friends at Quail Hollow. He did his homework and was prepared for each project he was working on and he expected you to do the same. In this way, he helped many people achieve more than they might have on their own. He was a loyal friend.

A few years ago, we convinced John to donate $42,000 from the Belk Foundation to support the Charlotte Uptown Rotary Club's World War II video project. Later, when the club wanted to expand the project I wouldn't go call on John again because I originally promised him it would be a one-time request. John called me after some of the other guys had made the request for more money. "Why weren't you with those guys?" John asked.

"Because I promised you it would be a onetime request," I responded.

"I didn't give them any money either," John said.

Shared by Chuck Prendergast, long-time friend of John:

John told me about the time he was at home watching television when an anonymous man called by telephone.

"Is this Mayor Belk?" he asked.

"Speaking," John replied.

"You are a damn SOB!" the man shouted.

"Anything else?" John asked.

"That's it," the man replied.

"Have a good day then," John replied and hung up.

Shared by Dr. John Kuykendall, former president of Davidson College:

I served as President of Davidson College from 1984 through 1997. John was on the Board of Trustees and was on the Executive Committee and the Presidential Search Committee.

During that search, he flew to Auburn University to visit with me and also with my family in our home. After the visit, I drove John back to the airport and sent him off through a terrible late winter thunderstorm. At that time we were a one-and-a-half car family with me driving a Volkswagen hatch back. John's knees were in his face, but he didn't complain. However, he never let me forget that it was the worst flight of his life. At the end of my annual review each year John said, 'Well, you've done a lot better than I thought you'd do!'

Once, when we were traveling together on a college fund raising trip I asked John how he handled all the contentious people during his terms of office as mayor. He explained that Bishop Spaugh of the Moravian Church and I think John's scout master advised, "When facing argumentative people, just think about the funniest thing that happened yesterday and put that expression on your face. It will drive them crazy!" John explained that is exactly what he tried to do.

I deeply appreciated John and always felt his support. He was a great note writer and always remembered birthdays.

Shared by Rolfe Neill, former publisher of *The Charlotte Observer*:

When I first came to Charlotte as publisher of *The Charlotte Observer*, John was serving as mayor. He called me, introduced himself, and said he would like to show me the town. At the designated time, he picked me up and drove directly to the water treatment plant. He explained the importance of water and then drove me to other important community resource sites and generally around Charlotte. I appreciated the fact that the mayor would take the time to show me around the city that he so loved.

John helped the city in so many ways, even down to introducing American Management Association courses to city employees. The expansion of the airport was perhaps the most important accomplishment and he is clearly the "father of our airport."

The Belk organization was the largest advertiser in *The Charlotte Observer* throughout his terms as mayor, but he never once sought to get preferential treatment to keep something out of or get something in the papers.

Shared by Luther Moore, senior vice president of Belk Stores Services:

John was a wise businessman. When in negotiations, John always cautioned me to never let them know we wanted anything. "Always let them think we're ready to walk away," he advised. He would never get into a deal with anyone who might have a character flaw. He believed that a person's name was better than silver and gold and he looked at a person's character even more closely than the deal. I think that is how he did so well in business.

Greed was never a motive for John.
He used to say that he only worked for Uncle Sam and his daddy, and his daddy paid better.

One time I suggested to John that Leroy Robinson was turning him into a lawyer. John replied, "Don't ever wish that on me!" John thought there were too many lawyers.

John's investment philosophy was, "Make the right decision in the first place and then don't look at it too often. You invest for the long term, stay patient, and don't worry about it." Sound advice I think.

Shared by Leighton Ford, Leighton Ford Ministries:

I have two special memories of John.

In 1983 I was asked to lead an area-wide evangelistic preaching series in the old coliseum, now Cricket Arena, with hundreds of churches in and surrounding Charlotte. The committee thought John would be the right person to lead the fund raising for the event. Bill Poe, who was chairing the committee, and I went to the old Belk Store offices downtown. John met us in their large conference room and he and his brother, Tom, sat at the head of the table. Another brother, Henderson, sat way back at the far end of the table. We sat down and Bill spelled out the goals of the crusade and asked John if he would lead the fund raising campaign.

John asked about the campaign goal, which was $225,000, a lot of money in those days. We talked a while, but John never really gave us a straight answer. I remember he said to me, "You just preach. Don't worry about money." The meeting was over.

We left the building and walked down the street, puzzled. Neither of us knew what he said. Just then, Tom came walking up behind us. We said in unison, "What did John say?"

"He said yes!" Tom replied. The money was raised.

❋ ❋ ❋

When we started the Leadership Breakfast Group, I went around town visiting with CEOs and senior partners of firms asking whether they thought the leadership group was a good idea. We had a first breakfast to talk about the concept and there were some mixed feelings about it. John was there, but he had to leave early. Before he left, he told us this story:

There were two old cowboys being chased by wild Indians. One of the cowboys had his horse shot out from under him. He got on behind the other one and the horse struggled along. The horse owner was worried that their pursuer might catch them and he asked the cowboy behind him what was happening to the Indian behind them. "Well, I'm not sure, but he's growing on me!"

With that, John said, "I have to go, but I think we should try this breakfast group and see if it grows on us." We never took a vote. John's story did the trick and we have been meeting for decades ever since.

At one of the last leadership group meetings John attended, I asked him if things had changed much in his lifetime. "Things are about the same in Charlotte from when I was young," he said. "Human beings don't change much. But the stores are doing better since Timmy took over."

Shared by Bill White, long-time friend of John:

John's wit and wisdom translated themselves into suggestions, answers, and even directives. Not unlike the Book of Proverbs, they called for the hearer to pause and contemplate the wisdom therein.

At times he sat in meetings with his eyes closed, but his mind was very much awake. I presided over a meeting where an employee matter was being discussed. Various members of the board discussed how to handle a very delicate situation, with no clear direction having evolved. As we went around the table, I asked John for his opinion.

He said, "Christmas is coming." He offered nothing more.
The discussion continued around the table until we reached John again. He repeated, "Christmas is coming."

I asked him to enlighten the rest of us and he said, "Christmas is coming. Santa's sleigh is going back empty and so is his bag. You put that fellow in the bag and you won't have to worry about him until next Christmas!"

John was committed, competitive, giving, humorous, and a visionary leader. He was sometimes confusing, but never confused. Some wise person once said, "For every ability, there is a responsibility, and for every responsibility, there is a judgment." Surely the abilities were within John Belk and surely he responded fully to them.

Shared by Sylvia Thompson, long-time friend of John:

Jack and I had the privilege of entertaining John and Claudia on several occasions at our Longboat Key home. Of course, the real entertainment always came from John. There was never a dull moment when John was present.

Our family and the Belks have mutual friends, Bob and Dottie Dickinson from Indianapolis. On one of the Belks' Longboat Key visits, the Dickinsons happened to be in residence in their home on Siesta. Naturally, we invited the Dickinsons to come over to dinner with us. It was a fun time for us all to be together. After dinner John got to his feet, thanked the Dickinsons for coming, and said, "Goodnight" and "Thank you for coming" even though he was not the host nor in his own home. Always a gentleman, John's remarks stunned Dottie.

Perhaps John's life motto was, "Early to bed, early to rise, makes a man healthy, wealthy, and wise." He certainly had health, wealth, and wisdom and we do miss him as well as his wit.

Shared by Bob Morgan, president of the Charlotte Chamber of Commerce:

A couple of years ago I asked John if he would speak to my son's Cub Scout group. He readily agreed and showed up on time one Sunday afternoon. John spoke about scouting and American history. He told the boys some of Charlotte's history, including George Washington's visit just after the War of the Revolution. When he was finished, one of the boys asked, "Mr. Belk, did you know George Washington?"

Shared by David Stovall, chairman, Belk, Inc. Central Division:

In 2007 I was assigned a project by John and was told he wanted it by a certain date. I worked hard on it, but didn't get it finished until around 7:30 p.m. on the designated due date. I decided to call John's office and leave him a voice mail that I had finished it, thereby not technically missing the deadline.

To my great surprise, John answered the phone. "Why, John, I didn't expect you to answer," I sputtered.

"Why did you call then?" John asked.

I was busted!

Shared by Andy Dulin, Charlotte City Council member:

John took a real interest in young people. After finishing my degree at Appalachian in 1984, I saw Claudia at the cleaners and she mentioned that John needed some younger friends. A few days later, John called me and invited me to play golf with him at Augusta National. We had a great time and went on a fairly regular basis. It was a sad day for me when John gave up golf.

John became an extra dad and mentor to me. This association taught me to be more thoughtful in many ways. "You'll write your obituary with your check book," he told me. "You make your mark in this world by what you give, not by what you take," he explained. He was masterful in helping me think about others and the community.

John and I always enjoyed sharing the Goodfellows' Club experience which helps needy people. I've now been a member for twenty-five years or more. We always sat together down front at the annual Goodfellows' fund raising luncheon. I always knew I would have some quality time with John even though we were in a room with 1200 other businessmen. Claudia lent me one of John's red sweaters that he wore to this event. I wore it with great pride at this past Goodfellows' luncheon.

❦ ❦ ❦

John helped determine the I85 and I77 placements and the airport expansion. His influence is legendary. His community leadership inspired me to run for public office. And, like most people who knew him, I thought of him as a best friend.

I invited John to a very small gathering of political supporters after winning a city council primary and he showed up. I was astonished that he would make the time to attend and said, "John, I'm so pleased to see you!"

"You invited me, didn't you?"

John was a master teacher by example.

Shared by Jim McNair:

One time John and I were driving to Charleston. John was riding shotgun and was asleep as far as I knew. "Crows have a free time," he said.

"What do you mean?" I asked.

"Look over there at those crows. They don't work at all. They are freeloaders."

Shared by Alex Coffin (in his book, *Brookshire and Belk, Businessmen in City Hall*, p. 238)**:**

In 1974 John and a majority of the city council and the county commission supported a consolidation of the city council and the county commission into one 18-member governing body. The vote was an overwhelming defeat. When asked why some opposed consolidation, Belk replied, "Well, I guess it's the reason the Lord didn't give a bullfrog wings. He just wants them to bump their fannies as they go along and others fly. Everyone is different you know . . ."

Shared by Darrell Williams:

In reviewing some of the transcripts of Howard Covington's 2003 interviews with John Belk for the company history books, I recently discovered some great comments by John in which he sums up some of the things that were most important to him.

"There are a lot of people that have given their lives for this organization (Belk) in making it what it is, and now it's made and we should keep it going."

"(What has given me the most satisfaction is) working with people. I've gotten more satisfaction out of it by working with the people on different matters."

"I never tried to be like daddy . . . I was just old John Belk and I couldn't be anybody else and I understand that. Why try to be somebody that you're not. It's enough if you get to know yourself, and like yourself."

[On finding contentment in life] "When you think back and you've been in two wars and had the privilege of being mayor of a city, and (you're part of) a great organization and have a lot of friends, I'd say I'm pretty lucky . . . A sense of humor and attitude are two of the best things you can develop. If your attitude is good and your sense of humor is good, and you believe in the Lord (and) that there's something bigger than what you are."

Shared by Tony Zeiss:

When I was Chairman of the Boy Scout Council's Executive Board, Luther Moore told me John was going to turn eighty years old on March 29, 2000. I thought it would be great for the council to throw a birthday party for John in appreciation for his years of service and support. Others agreed with me, including Leroy Mayne, Executive Director of our local council. The two of us set up a meeting with John to get his permission to have the party. After the pleasantries, I told John what we were there for and that we would like his permission to hold the event.

John acted as if he didn't hear me and then asked, "Tony, where are you going to leave your money?" I was flabbergasted and tried to connect the two thoughts, but couldn't. I recovered by saying Beth and I would leave our money to our boys, our church, and the Boy Scouts.

"What about Central Piedmont?" he shot back.

I was stunned and quickly said that it was simply an oversight and that Central Piedmont would certainly get its fair share.

John then began pointing out his trophy animal mounts from a month-long safari he'd taken in Kenya. He talked about how they camped, told us about the world record oryx he had taken and shared a few stories about his lion and other animals located around his office. It took another thirty minutes to get John back to the original question and he finally said it would be fine.

We held the birthday celebration at Founders Hall uptown and over 400 of his friends and family attended. Representative Eagle Scouts with flags flying attended from almost every troop in town. It was a huge success and we were honored to be able to celebrate the life and eightieth birthday of such a renowned scout.

I have never forgotten John's penetrating question, which underscored his belief that we make a life by what we give.

A year or so back, I asked John to tell me about the major generational changes he had experienced. "I haven't seen too many, beyond those that are technological. Human nature is the same as it always has been. But I still get my news from the newspaper, Claudia gets hers mostly from the television, and Mary Claudia gets hers from the Internet!"

❉ ❉ ❉

For the past few years, a group of us have been promoting the concept of creating a Charlotte Trail of History which would place bronze statues of key historical figures of Mecklenburg County along the metropolitan section of the Little Sugar Creek Greenway. Chase Saunders, Allen Tate, Tommy and Patty Norman, and the May 20th Society leaders Charles Jonas, George Dewey, Mary Claudia (Belk) Pilon, Meg McElwain, and others have been raising funds to build the first statue which will be a representation of Captain James Jack and his horse. James Jack took the Mecklenburg Declaration of Independence and the Mecklenburg Resolves by horseback up to the Continental Congress in Philadelphia in June of 1775. By almost any standard, James Jack is our most celebrated historical figure and that is why his statue is being built first. He and his father operated a very popular tavern at Trade and Church Streets downtown. With this one courageous ride, James Jack became Charlotte's Paul Revere.

John Belk loved history and he contributed generously to the fund for Captain Jack's statue. I saw John just a few days after he made his financial pledge and thanked him for his generosity.

"He was a bartender," John remarked with that little grin and twinkling eyes.

∾ Chapter Four ∾

Quoting John Montgomery Belk

Every once in a long while, we encounter a person who is easily remembered, identified, and loved for his or her expressions. John Belk is right up there in the quotable category with Abraham Lincoln, Yogi Berra, and Mark Twain. I have been collecting his quotes for over fifteen years and other people have been gathering them for much longer. This brief chapter is designed to provide a fairly comprehensive list of John's most memorable quotes, though it is doubtful we could ever discover all of his witticisms and one-liners. Many people gave me the same quotes so it was impossible to credit everyone. Please learn from and enjoy them.

THE WORLD ACCORDING TO JOHN BELK

Prepared for John's retirement celebration, May 25, 2004

"Some people drink from the fountain of knowledge, others just gargle."

"Regardless of what you do, your mother and your dog will always put up with you."

"I feel as if this is a void we have lacked in the past."

"On responsibility, I know what a big shoulder it is."

"We ought to decide where our problems are and implement our own."

"My words might have been the wisdom for your knowledge."

"I think you're getting into something you don't want to get out of."

"She's her mother's apple."

"Tell us what it is and we'll know whether we didn't get it or not."

"My favorite part of politics is meeting the flesh."

"Zoning is one of the most important things whether we are right or wrong."

"You can't be unreasonable about something until you get the facts."

"Charlotte's key to the city may not be as eloquent as others."

"Charlotte is behind on its future."

"Will there be any mediums in the new expressway?"

"This would solve the solution."

"On school desegregation, the thing I'm scared of, and this is what we've been trying to stress, is education."

"That is not deductive to good planning."

"I always get a little mixed up when I have to stop and think."

"Sometimes I get so far out in left field, I run out of grass."

"Sometimes I'm in left field and we're on the basketball court."

"You don't have to confuse me because I don't know enough about it to be confused."

Provided by contributors to this book and from Susan Jetton's and the editor's collections:

"As you slide down the banister of life, may the splinters always point in the right direction."

"I can keep a secret. It's just those people I tell it to that can't."

"Life is like a roll of toilet paper, the closer you get to the end, the faster it goes."

"I don't have any problem with Charlotte's traffic, except for those people who get in my way."

"He's the worst patient man in the world because he's never used any."

"Fat possums run late."

"Don't get into a fight with your newspaper. They will write your obituary."

"Don't bother telling other people your problems, half of 'em won't care and the other half will be glad you've got 'em."

"Those people don't have inferiority complexes, they're just inferior."

"There are two times when a man doesn't understand women. Before he gets married and after he gets married."

"I tell the devil, 'Get behind me and don't push.'"

"You've got to be a good follower before you can be a good leader."

"Is this the census of opinion?"

"I'm not clear enough on it to ask you any questions, much less tell you what to do."

"You give me the impression that you're educated beyond your ability."

"An ugly win is better than an ugly loss."

"You've already written another chapter in a new book and I'm still on *Gone with the Wind*."

"I think it ought to be a two-way street. Otherwise, don't come back down the street."

"I've been mixed up with the alphabet ever since Roosevelt was elected President."

When a wine glass spilled John would say, "That wine glass isn't house broken."

"It's confusing, we park in the driveway and drive on the parkway."

"If you don't know where you're going, any road will get you there."

"Indoor plumbing is one of the greatest contributions to civilization and it's so much cleaner."

"In a deck, you've got 52 cards. And when you've got one up, you can see that card and you know what it is."

"Trains don't fly and you ain't going to speed them up much."

"It's all right to let a dog chew on a bone out in the yard, but when he's in a house chewing on a bone and the bone is still in your leg, it's time you did something about it."

"Even if it is in the country, a raw diamond is still rough."

"Just tighten up the shoestrings and the shoes won't fall off the feet."

"If we're not ready to spear the bullfrog before he jumps into the pond, it's gonna be gone."

"Well, I reckon that's better than falling in a septic hole."

"Charlotte's still the finest city in the county outside the city limits."

"Gun control is too much like a dictatorship."

"The Lord expects more of Charlotte than of other cities 'cause he tests us so much more."

"Nobody seems to like a street in their front door."

"They are forming a meeting that we can have later."

"This is the point I wanted him to bring up on this so we would not be confused about that."

"The governor's going to announce Friday that he's going to appoint a committee to revamp the state because the state is out!"

"Get some peanuts over to the county commission. Some of them are cracking and some of them aren't."

"Those striking sanitation workers will be persecuted to the fullest extent."

"The first time I turned on cable TV, I thought I was constipated."

"I would hate to see this thing 'cause it's so much of an enjoyment."

"I don't want you to have a guilty complex."

"I'm glad I've just got athlete's problems 'cause all I have to do is scratch."

"The trouble is, we have them in their stalls but now we've got to keep them from backing out before the race."

"This is a false nomer. They keep putting the monkey on our back down here and we don't have a cage to put it in."

Chapter Five
Parting Thoughts

John Montgomery Belk was a complex individual who was beloved by almost everyone he knew. He had private dinners with many presidents of our country and governors of our state. He fraternized with the most important business leaders of his time. He guided the development and growth of our city through sometimes tumultuous political periods, yet he remained steadfast in his purpose to live a God-centered life. He loved his family, the Boy Scouts, his business, his country, and his community. John just loved people.

Family
In a Howard Covington Jr. interview in 2001, John stated. "I've been pretty lucky all of my life to have good people around to help me out. Claudia helped me out in particular. She helped me get elected. I have a nice wife and a lovely daughter."

Boy Scouts
John joined the Boy Scouts when he was twelve years old and advanced through the ranks until he became an Eagle Scout on November 28, 1947. While serving in the Korean War, he organized several Boy Scout troops and upon his return, John was a Scout Master and later, an Explorer Scout Advisor. He served as president of the Mecklenburg Council of the Boy Scouts in 1960-61, president of the Southeast Region for Scouting in 1990-92, and was vice president of the National Council in 1981. He received the top local, regional, and national awards for adult scout leaders.

Business
John rose to great heights in the department store business. Darrell Williams, a long time Belk employee and archivist, had this to say about John's business career when he wrote John's obituary: "John Belk served with character and distinction as the chief executive officer of the Belk department store organization for more than fifty years. His vision and leadership resulted in the development and growth of Belk into the nation's largest privately-owned department store company with more than 300 stores across sixteen southern states.

His career was characterized by many extraordinary achievements and outstanding contributions to his company, the retail industry, and his community. He served as a model of integrity, honesty, and fairness throughout his life." John also served as Chair of the National Retail Federation.

Country
John, along with all of his brothers, served in World War II. He was redeployed to Korea and served as an officer mostly with a United Nations unit whose mission was to help rebuild South Korean communities. Although John experienced combat, he spent most of his time helping Koreans build businesses and rebuild their communities.

City
John served four two-year terms as Charlotte's mayor from 1969 to 1977 helping the city emerge into one of the most dynamic cities for business, families, and education in the nation. John and his colleagues ushered in the foundations of this 'New South City' that included a visionary transportation system, one of the best airports in the country, big league sports, bigger and better parks, and did all this through the challenging period of Civil Rights, which he supported. Throughout the rest of his life John was affectionately referred to as 'Mr. Mayor.'

John was very generous with his time and his wealth. Wanting to support every good cause with his time, he also supported most of them with his money. He supported private and public education at every level, most notably, Davidson College, his alma mater. He supported Boy Scouts, theater, historical events, greenways, and about anything else that he thought would be good for the people of this community.

People
His was a life well lived, a life with an enduring purpose because he loved people. In August 2001, John was asked by Howard E. Covington, "When you think back about fifty years, what gives you the most satisfaction?"

"Working with people. Like working in the mayor's office, I got more satisfaction out of it by working with the people on different matters. You can get along with anybody, but you set your goals and then don't worry about yourself. And that's what we did in this organization (Belk) and what we did in the city. I don't know of anything I've done in this organization or the city by myself. It's the people with whom I've associated that really deserve the credit, not me."

Chuck Prendergast contributed this last and fitting story about our friend:

Several years back, John, Claudia, Gretchen, and I drove downtown for an evening event at the Belk Theater. John parked behind Discovery Place and we all walked up toward Tryon Street. Claudia and Gretchen were slightly ahead of John and me. Our wives were crossing Tryon Street when John noticed a man who was lying in the street several yards away.

Upon seeing this, John stepped into the street and held up his hand to stop traffic, then inspected the man. He then rolled the man up onto the sidewalk. With that, he gestured for traffic to continue, dusted off his hands, and we proceeded to the theater.

John rejoined me and said, "He needs to quit drinking so much!"

❖ ❖ ❖

Editor's Note: I was privileged to be a member of the Leighton Ford Leadership group with John for over fifteen years. This remarkable group of men meets once a month to study the word of God, share their Christian journeys together, and provide mentoring to rising young leaders each Christmas season. We take turns teaching each month's lesson, usually from the Bible or from a book written about the Bible.

At our April 2007 meeting, Leighton Ford reminded us that John would be presenting the lesson from our book at the May meeting. John said, "I'll be speaking on love." That wasn't the theme of the next chapter in the book we were studying, but Leighton abdicated without the slightest protest and quickly said, "And John will be speaking to us on the subject of love.

On May 2, 2007, John spoke to us about the four types of love, that being Eros, Philia, Storge, and Agape. John had evidently researched his topic well and he had hand written notes that he occasionally followed. It was very clear that he wanted us to know that love of family, others, and God was a priority in his life and should be in ours.

At one point he made the point that our human nature can be contrary to our will to love. He illustrated by relating the following story:

"When I was on patrol in Korea once, our truck ran over a little girl. She was still alive and we did what we could for her then drove her to the local hospital. We left and drove out of town.

That evening we ran into some guerrillas on a hill top. We killed several of them and took the hill. As I lay there, I couldn't stop thinking about that girl and how we kept her alive with our concern and love. Yet, just a few hours later we were killing these men. This was a real contrast. In the eyes of the Lord, it doesn't make any sense. Even today, I don't know how to figure that out. How you could try saving a life one moment and taking lives the next?"

Sadly, John physically passed away just a few weeks after this contemplative lesson. Leighton asked all of us at our next Leadership Group meeting to write a sentence or two about our dear friend, John Belk, so he could share them with Claudia. This is what they had to say:

Peter Browning:

John never forgot a name. He also never forgot to say thank you. And he was the most articulate inarticulate communicator ever!

Andy Calhoun:

John's work and leadership, his vision for this community, will be a legacy for generations. He was and will continue to be a blessing to this community.

Robert Cooley:

John's many written notes always brought joy and hope. He was an encourager . . . a modern day Barnabas.

Larry Dagenhart:

John and I disagreed a number of times, but I always knew where he stood. And I know for sure that he loved God, his church, Davidson College, and his city. He was a positive force in all of those relationships.

Leighton Ford:

I think of mythical characters when I think of John. Like the Sphinx, he spoke truth in riddles. Like Hercules, he had big shoulders to carry many things. And like Solomon, (not a myth) he was wise. He was shrewd about people, but not cynical. How thankful I am to have known him.

Peter Gilchrist:

I never asked John for help that he didn't respond positively. When he helped, he would do it in unanticipated ways, often writing letters and making phone calls to people I didn't know." (John was Peter's Boy Scout leader)

Frank Harrison:

John was always there for me. Soon after we came to Charlotte, John reached out to our family and has been a great friend ever since. I thank God for his life. I loved John very much. I'm missing him and keep expecting him to walk in five minutes late to our office at Coca-Cola.

Jim Morgan:

John never failed to speak, call you by name, and make you feel that you were important to him. He was a mentor to many of us without ever realizing what he was giving. Whenever I think of John, I smile and I have a warm feeling envelop me as if he had just made one of his unique and wonderful observations.

Bill White:

We respond in gratitude to God for the gifts of love, leadership, and humor of John Montgomery Belk, a wonderfully gifted man who shared those gifts so freely in responsive service to his Lord.

Bill Vandiver:

John was a man who truly made a difference in the world! He was a man of great wisdom with a passion for life who helped people from all parts of the community live a better life. He left a legacy of good that few have done.

Charlie Zeigler:

John was so special. Now he's in heaven with that great big heart and grin of his. He was so good to me, like a loving big brother. He made me a better person with his examples of integrity, wit, and love for others. What a life you two were fortunate to have together!

Tony Zeiss:

John was a wonderful friend, mentor, and example for me. His love of family, community, Christ, and his fellow man was truly exemplary! I loved the guy!

❆ ❆ ❆

We're told in the second chapter of James that even though Christians are saved by grace and faith, "Faith without works is dead." Indeed, faith is perfected by our works. John Belk was a wonderful example of a committed Christian who put all of his heart and talents to work for others and God's kingdom.

I once asked all the men in our Leighton Ford Leadership group to reflect upon their purpose in life and write their epitaphs. An epitaph conveys the core desire of one's heart, its dominant purpose, and for what they most want to be remembered. John Montgomery Belk might easily have claimed that he was a nationally prominent businessman, a nationally prominent policy maker, or a nationally prominent Boy Scout leader, but he didn't.

On the next page you can see what he wrote:

"He was known as a man who sought Christ."

– John Montgomery Belk

Appendices

Appendix I
John Belk essay, *I Like Calling Charlotte, North Carolina, Home*

Appendix II
John Belk Obituary

Appendix III
John Belk tribute, The Giving Heart Award

Appendix IV
Additional reading sources on John Belk

Appendix I

I Like Calling Charlotte, North Carolina, Home
by John M. Belk
December 1999

The familiar words "nothing could be finer than to be in Carolina" hold true for me and countless others who grew up in this state and are fortunate to call it home. However, as a native Charlottean, I would add to this verse, "Nothing could be finer than to be in Charlotte, North Carolina."

I can't adequately describe all the good things about my hometown. The superlatives abound. I can only say that there's no other place like it, and I'm proud to call it home.

I have had a 79-year love affair with Charlotte, and I am truly blessed to live in what I believe is the best part of the world with the most wonderful and gracious people. It has been both amazing and fulfilling to witness Charlotte's rise to prominence as the largest city in the Carolinas and a shining star among the nation's cities.

I have many cherished memories of growing up in Charlotte, and I have been privileged to play a role in the city's dramatic progress and growth over the years as chairman of the Belk department store organization, a former mayor of Charlotte, and an actively involved business and civic leader.

I remember fondly my childhood years when I lived in our home on Hawthorne Lane, near what used to be called Presbyterian Hospital. This is where my beloved parents—William Henry Belk and Mary Irwin Belk—raised me and my four brothers and sister: Henry, Sarah (Gambrell), Irwin, Henderson and Tom.

My father spent lots of time "at the store," and my mother took care of us and ran the house. We looked forward to our family times together, especially on Christmas holidays and birthdays. It was always a treat to go downtown to see the Christmas lights and store window decorations at Belk's, Ivey's, Montaldo's and Efird's. Of course, Belk's were always the best.

I will never forget how dedicated my father was to his family, business, religion and community. He and my mother gave us a good Presbyterian upbringing, and instilled in us a strong work ethic and a sense of civic pride and responsibility.

I inherited my mother's love of history. She was an active leader in the Daughters of the American Revolution and the Colonial Dames, and supported the preservation and restoration of local historic sites, such as the Hezekiah Alexander house. Charlotte's rich history helps define who we are and how the city has become what it is today.

For example, the bold, "can-do" spirit of Charlotte's citizens can be traced back to 1775, when a group of Mecklenburg County's Scotch-Irish settlers signed a declaration of independence from Britain—15 months before the signing of the American declaration. Five years later, British General Cornwallis and his troops fought a bitter skirmish at the Battle of Charlotte, and after a brief occupation the distressed commander said he found "a rebel behind ever bush" and described the town and its people as "a veritable nest of hornets."

I experienced Charlotte's progressive spirit most directly as head of the Chamber of Commerce in 1964, and later, when I served as Charlotte's mayor from 1969 to 1977, and as a member of the Airport Advisory Committee. Charlotte's business and government leaders, supported by citizens, worked together to bring about an unprecedented era of progress and growth, which continues today.

Improvements were made on many fronts, thanks to the commitment and involvement of many citizens from throughout the Charlotte community. During my tenure as mayor, we strengthened our infrastructure by building new roads and paving the way for expansion of the airport. We saved millions of dollars by improving the city's credit rating from AA to AAA. A new convention center was built uptown, along with five new bank towers, which showed Charlotte's emergence as a great financial center.

Three major retail malls were constructed—at SouthPark, Eastland and the Overstreet mall downtown. The Discovery Place science museum, Spirit Square, and 16 new neighborhood parks also opened.

In December, 1977, after serving as Charlotte's mayor for 8 ½ years, I decided not to run for another term. My tenure as mayor was one of the most exciting and rewarding times of my life, and even though I have continued to serve on numerous civic boards and committees, this was the highlight of my public service.

When I left the mayor's office, I told Charlotte citizens: "I wish I were capable of expressing in words my feeling of solemn pride at having been so honored and trusted as mayor of Charlotte. Charlotte has been good to me, and it will be my eternal hope to be remembered as someone who was good to Charlotte. This city is much more than vast areas of residences and towering buildings. The greatest asset of Charlotte by far is its good people. I shall always do whatever I can to help make Charlotte one of the best places in the land, and to that end shall always offer the best hopes of my mind, my heart and my soul."

There are numerous reasons why so many people and businesses have been attracted to Charlotte in recent years. It's a beautiful place to live, with its canopy of trees, flowering dogwoods and azaleas in the spring; attractive neighborhoods with charming homes; and outstanding schools and colleges, such as the University of North Carolina at Charlotte, Central Piedmont Community College, Johnson C. Smith University, and Queens College. It also boasts an excellent public library, a good hospital and health care system, and an exciting array of professional sports, including the Carolina Panthers, the Charlotte Hornets, the Charlotte Checkers, the Charlotte Sting and the legendary stock car racing events at Lowe's Motor Speedway.

Additionally, Charlotte is loved for its many churches, outstanding restaurants, award-winning museums, cultural arts programs, and the list goes on.

Charlotte has a long-standing, far-reaching reputation as a good place to do business. This is primarily the result of the city's excellent Chamber of Commerce and the positive relationships maintained among business, civic and government leaders. Charlotte leaders historically have put the good of the city and its citizens above politics and self-interest.

The city's sparkling uptown skyline, which features the impressive office towers of Bank of America, First Union, Wachovia, Branch Banking and Trust Company, Duke Energy, Transamerica, and others, is just a snapshot of the strength and vitality of Charlotte's business community. The city is now a base for many leading companies, including B.F. Goodrich, Ruddick Corp., IBM, Nucor Corp., United Dominion Industries, Inc., Lance, Inc., Glenayre Technologies, Inc., Piedmont Natural Gas Co., Coca-Cola Bottling Co. Consolidated, and many others. It has also become a growing international city, with more than 340 foreign firms located here.

Perhaps the biggest catalysts for Charlotte's rapid growth have been its interstate highways and its airport. Last year, Charlotte/Douglas International Airport was ranked 35th in the world in total passengers, with nine major airlines handling nearly 11.5 million passenger boardings. Upon completion of its new runway, the airport will become one of the largest and best equipped in the country.

Our city continues to grow by leaps and bounds. Nearly everywhere you look, there are signs of a strong economy and a good business climate. Along with this progress, however, have come many new issues and challenges that must be addressed, such as traffic, education, diversity, crime and others. It is my hope that through good planning, effective public debate and dialogue, and a continued strong partnership between business and government, Charlotte will overcome its obstacles and have a bright future.

This will require Charlotte's citizens to revisit and gain a renewed appreciation for the city's history and culture. We must rekindle some of the Southern hospitality and good manners that helped make Charlotte the gem of the South that it is today and the great place that I am so proud to call home.

Appendix II

In Memory of John Montgomery Belk
1920–2007

We mourn the loss of John Montgomery Belk, business leader, public servant and philanthropist, who gave generously of himself for the betterment of the Charlotte community, the state and world.

John Belk served with character and distinction as the chief executive officer of the Belk department store organization for more than 50 years. His vision and leadership resulted in the development and growth of Belk into the nation's largest privately-owned department store company with more than 300 stores across 16 Southern states. His career was characterized by many extraordinary achievements and outstanding contributions to his company, the retail industry and his community, and he served as a model of integrity, honesty and fairness throughout his life.

He was born in Charlotte, North Carolina, on March 29, 1920, to the late Mary Irwin Belk and William Henry Belk, founder of Belk department stores, and attended Charlotte public schools, McCallie School in Chattanooga, Tennessee, and subsequently Davidson College in Davidson, North Carolina, where he received a Bachelor of Science degree in economics in 1943. He also served his country honorably in the U.S. Army infantry during World War II from 1943 to 1945, attaining the rank of Lieutenant, and was recalled to active duty in Korea from 1950 to 1952.

For more than 50 years he worked in close partnership with his brother, the late Thomas M. Belk, former president of Belk stores, to strengthen the company and position it for future growth and success, and together they led the transformation of Belk stores from bargain stores in downtown locations to modern fashion stores in major shopping centers and regional malls throughout the South.

John Belk's parents instilled in him a deep sense of obligation to civic involvement, community service and philanthropy that resulted in his involvement in many key leadership roles on the local, state and national levels, including his service as president of the Charlotte Chamber of Commerce and as mayor of the City of Charlotte for eight and one-half years from 1969 to 1977. As Charlotte's mayor, he presided over an unprecedented period of growth and prosperity during which Charlotte became a thriving city and major center for finance, commerce and air transportation, and his administration set a positive example of how business and government can work together to build a better community.

John Belk provided decisive leadership and wise counsel to numerous corporations, business and professional groups, and civic, educational, charitable and religious organizations throughout his career, serving in such positions as chairman of The Belk Foundation; board member and past chairman of the National Retail Federation; member of the Davidson College board of trustees; member of the University of North Carolina at Charlotte board of visitors; member and past president of the Presbyterian Hospital Foundation, and member and Elder at Myers Park Presbyterian Church, to name a few.

John Belk was a long-time member and leader in the Boy Scouts of America who has been awarded many top Scouting honors and designations, including Baden-Powell Fellow, Distinguished Eagle Scout, the Silver Beaver, the Silver Antelope and the Silver Buffalo, and has held top Scouting posts, including president of the BSA Southeast Region and member of the advisory council of the BSA National Executive Board.

John Belk received numerous awards and honors recognizing his outstanding civic leadership, community service and philanthropy, and has been one of the Charlotte region's strongest sports advocates who played a key role in bringing major collegiate sporting events and professional sports teams to Charlotte, including the former NBA Charlotte Hornets basketball team and the NFL Carolina Panthers football team.

John Belk was a devoted husband, father and grandfather, respectively, to his wife of 36 years, Claudia Watkins Belk, his daughter, Mary Claudia Pilon, and his three grandchildren, (James Montgomery Pilon, John Michael Pilon, and Katherine Belk Pilon).

When John Belk left the mayor's office in December, 1977, he told *The Charlotte Observer*, "I wish I were capable of expressing in words my feeling of solemn pride at having been so honored and trusted as mayor of Charlotte. Charlotte has been good to me, and it will be my eternal hope to be remembered as someone who was good to Charlotte. This city is much more than vast areas of residences and towering buildings. The greatest asset of Charlotte by far is its good people. I shall always do whatever I can to help make Charlotte one of the best places in the land, and to that end shall always offer the best hopes of my mind, my heart, and my soul."

John Belk cared deeply for his company, his community, his church, and his family. We celebrate his life and cherish his memory. Our hearts go out to his family and all who knew and loved him.

– Darrell Williams

Appendix III

The Giving Heart Award
John Montgomery Belk
November 15, 2007

Anyone who has lived in Charlotte in, say, the past 50 years is well acquainted with John Belk. He was a major figure in this community's life, business, government, politics, social and educational and religious enterprises. We have a freeway and buildings and scholarships which bear his name; and that's to say nothing of a larger than life personality which has yielded a myriad of good stories, and his special way of using the language which was usually memorable though not always intelligible.

John Belk has been and will be legendary in this town and beyond, and the wonderful recollections of his full life are the sort that last. Even if you never met him, you likely feel as though you've known the man. Growing up here in the 1940s and 50s, I surely felt that way; though the first time I actually met him face-to-face was early in 1984 when he came to my home in Auburn, Alabama with a small contingent of folks from Davidson College. As I recall—and John would never let me forget—we nearly killed him twice in one short evening: First, we crammed his 6 foot four inch frame into the backseat of an ancient VW hatchback, for a "toad's wild ride" through our lovely village. Second, we sent him and his crowd off on a charter place into the teeth of one of those wild and unpredictable winter thunder storms in Alabama for what he often called the worst flight of his life.

Good thing for me that John didn't seem to bear a grudge: thereafter he was one of my "bosses" for the next thirteen years! And maybe in part because of that first encounter every year at the end of my annual review John said exactly the same thing: "Well," he'd say, "you did a lot better than I thought you were going to do!" which I eventually took to be more-than-adequate praise from one who became a treasured mentor and friend.

John Belk, it is frequently and truly said, was a rainmaker for this community and beyond, a key figure in the transformation of Charlotte from the sleepy overgrown town of his boyhood into the vibrant city it is today. A major aspect of John's contribution to that metamorphosis was his special capacity to foster good causes in which he believed. He was gifted with a proper balance of generosity and hard-nosed acumen about the ways in which people and institutions work. In choosing him for the Giving Heart Award, this organization has showed eminent good judgment; maybe even better judgment than we can know.

Certainly we all know that John was a person of great generosity. In my experience—and I'm sure others here would verify this—John's understanding of philanthropy and his willingness to follow that understanding with personal engagement and action was an aspect of his character which grew and continued to grow throughout his long life. One of the most gratifying aspects of his later years must surely have been his sheer delight at seeing institutions and programs he had fostered come alive and bear fruit.

Beyond that marvelous personal record on generosity, though, I am convinced that we do not/cannot yet fully appreciate the impact of John's precept and example upon many others, peers and contemporaries and beyond, who are or will become possessed of "giving hearts" because of his example.

John Belk had the providential inclination and capacity to give himself, but he also had an equally providential gift for encouraging others to be generous. In following his leadership as chair of a fairly ambitious campaign, I was privileged to observe and, I hope, to learn from John as a qualified grand master at the art of opening the hearts and pocketbooks of others. Any request he made of others for their benevolence was quite difficult to misunderstand or ignore—even in Belkese—because it was authenticated by the intentions and actions embodied in John's own generosity. And that's just a plain fact.

So I suggest to those who made this choice and to all of you who are participants in the sponsoring society, that not only have you done well, you have almost certainly done better than we can know in choosing John Montgomery Belk as this year's recipient of the Giving Heart Award.

When John retired as mayor thirty years ago next month, he said the following in his farewell statement to the Observer: "It will be my eternal hope to be remembered as someone who was good to Charlotte." Today we agree that John's hope was fulfilled, not only with respect to this community which he loved, but in the larger community of humankind.

Indeed, in my mind's eye I can almost picture an encounter a few weeks back in which St. Peter opened the gate extra wide and said, "Well, John, you did a lot better than I thought you'd do!"

– John W. Kuykendall

Appendix IV

Read more about John Belk, from Darrell Williams

One of my favorite roles at Belk has been that of "resident historian." Over the years, this has involved coordinating the publication of several books:

> ***Belk: A Century of Retail Leadership*** was written by Howard E. Covington and published by The University of North Carolina Press in 1988 in conjunction with the company's 100th anniversary.
>
> In 1994, the University of North Carolina at Charlotte published, ***Brookshire and Belk, Businessmen in City Hall***, by Alex Coffin, which chronicles the administrations of Stan Brookshire and John Belk who served as mayors of Charlotte
>
> In ***Belk: The Company and the Family That Built It***, published in 2004, Covington updates the first book to include the events leading up to the consolidation of Belk's corporate structure into Belk, Inc. and the subsequent strategic moves that positioned the company for future growth.

These books are recommended reading to those who want to learn more about John Belk and the history of Belk. There's also a company history exhibit at the Belk corporate office that displays hundreds of artifacts, photos and documents telling the rich history of the Belk family and company.

Index

Babb, Jim	46	McCrory, Pat	44
Battle, Bishop George	32, 47, 94	McNair, Jim	59, 74, 87, 108
Belk, Claudia	10, 17, 69, 71, 73, 77, 78, 79, 80, 91, 134	Medlin, John	58
		Moore, Luther	46, 94, 103, 110
		Morgan, Bob	107
Belk, Johnny	11, 19, 85, 98	Morgan, Jim	124
Belk, Katherine	20, 134	Morris, Katie Belk	23
Belk, Tim	11, 22	Myrick, Sue	56
Browning, Peter	122	Neil, Rolfe	94, 103
Byers, Debra	31, 36	Norman, Tommy	9, 57, 111
Calhoun, Andy	123	Orr, Jerry	59, 94
Cannon, Carol M.	37	Pilon, Mary Claudia Belk	10, 14, 18, 20, 23, 26, 52, 57, 71, 73, 80, 111, 134
Coffin, Alex	9, 93, 95, 109, 139		
Cooley, Robert	123		
Crowell, Belinda	35	Pittenger, Robert	43, 48, 74, 91
Crowell, Dottie	45	Pitts, Ralph	9, 94, 100
Dagenhart, Larry	123	Prendergast, Chuck	102, 121
Dalton, Bob	48, 66	Prendergast, Gretchen	56
Dickson, Stuart	31, 43, 51, 86	Purgason, Paulette	39
Disher, Bill	87, 95	Robinson, Leroy	28, 36, 79, 84, 91, 96, 104
Dulin, Andy	107		
Erwin, Mark	59, 86, 74	Robinson, Carrie	29
Fettner, Ann	95	Rogers, Bob	49
Ford, Leighton	104, 121, 123, 125	Rose, Louis	22, 51, 89
		Stovall, David	107
Gambrell, Sarah Belk	20	Thompson, Sydnor	90
Gantt, Harvey	89	Thompson, Sylvia	106
Gilchrist, Peter	123	Thorne, Tod	62
Haggai, Tom	54	Vandiver, Bill	124
Hampton, Frances Killian	35	Vangen, Colonel Terry	30
Harris, Cammie	62, 85	Wallace, Mason	40
Harris, Johnny	30, 51, 87	Weisiger, Ed	55
Harrison, Frank	124	Wentz, Meb	24
Jamison, Susan	37, 89	Wheeler, Humpy	99
Jetton, Susan	33, 114	White, Bill	105, 124
Johnson, Jay	51	William, Chris	87
Killian, Ray	11, 60, 101	Williams, Darrell	10, 109, 119, 135, 139
Kimbrell, Duke	51		
Knight, Sally Gambrell	21	Williams, Nancy	27
Kuykendall, Dr. John	43, 102, 138	Zeigler, Charlie	124
Matthews, Frank	61	Zeiss, Tony	12, 79, 81, 95, 110, 125
Mayne, Leroy	63, 110		
McCaskill, John	42	Zimmerman, David	91
McColl, Hugh	31, 99	Zimmerman, Joan	47, 92